# LESSONS FROM MY TIME WITH THE BOTTLE

AF439540

Derrick How

Copyright Page

Lessons From My Time With The Bottle, Copyright © 2024 by Derrick How.

All rights reserved.

No part of this publication may be reproduced, distributed, or transmitted in any form or by any means, including photocopying, recording, or other electronic or mechanical methods, without the prior written permission of the publisher, except as permitted by U.S. copyright law. For permission requests, contact me at [email] or via my website: www.LessonsFromTheBottle.com.

# Dedication

To my sons, who mean everything to me. It is my greatest hope you will learn a few lessons from me which serve you well in life.

# Contents

# 1 | | Mangled but Fixable

*Action expresses priorities.*
> **—Mahatma Gandhi**

Almost there, I thought. It wasn't easy relying on the doctor-prescribed cane to hold my unsteady weight. My body screamed out at me like I was attacking it. It didn't matter because I was determined to make the trek across the lawn to the shed. It wasn't far away, but it might as well have been a mile. Retreating back to the safety of my house would have been easier, not to mention the easy way out. My nagging inner voice told me to work past the pain—after all, it was my own damn fault—and it insisted I move onward, so I did. It was my day to face what was in that shed and bring the shielded mystery out into the light.

With each step taken, I assessed what was wrong with me. Every breath of the beautiful, fresh coastal air made my ribs scream out in discomfort. The weight on my ankle made me hunch over a bit, casting a crooked shadow on the lush green grass in front of me. I looked like an old man and felt like one too, despite only being forty-three. But the sun above me was shining down, and the day was beautiful by all accounts. The Monterey Peninsula is this type of place.

The doors to the shed were sturdy and resilient to the blowing winds but were still weathered from the tough years of enduring the ocean air. Compared to me, whose very presence felt like a disruption, it was easy to see that the toughest demon I was facing at that moment was me. Haven't we all been there in life a time or two? Or, in my case, on an endless repeat loop for a whole lot of years. I leaned forward and reached for the shed's handle, swinging the door open. The sun's rays behind me cast their light into the small building and over to the corner. There it was, my nemesis and reminder—a blue mangled frame to my cruiser e-bike. Yeah, it had been in a rough accident that just happened to have me riding it at the time. Separating myself from that bike frame was mostly a way to avoid acknowledging my part in that accident. I say mostly because I could have slipped off that steep edge and down the deep rutty pit even if I had not been drinking. I thought I was okay, but the test told a different tale, one where some guy rode his bike off the edge of a cliff with a .29 blood alcohol content, something they discovered when they extracted my body from the bottom. Strangely, this was still not my personal rock bottom, although the rocks piercing into my mangled body might dispute this if they could. They had done their job and left me with quite a list of broken parts: a femur, ulna, radius, clavicle, five ribs, plus a fractured sternum and four back fractures.

One would think staring down the twisted frame of my near demise would be enough to startle some sense into me. That day had almost cost me my life, and much to my surprise, despite all my challenges and self-perceptions, I preferred life to what came next. And when it came to Heaven versus Hell, I was definitely headed south, if you get my drift. Not because I was bad but because I let my weakness consume me more times than I could either admit or remember. There was still time to turn it around.

I looked over to a dark corner of the musty-smelling shed and knew my next move. My cane dropped to the floor, landing with a dull thud, and I started to move across the floor. My foot slid after me, leaving a snake-like trail to show where I was headed. I began moving around the old paint cans, which helped me hide my stash of booze bottles. They were everywhere, and if it hadn't been for the fact that no one usually entered that shed besides me, they would not have been there. It was a favorite hiding spot. Somehow, when I went to the "shed" to get something, I never came back quite the same.

A new day, a new beginning. I was going to make it happen. These positive thoughts were forced, but it was a sudden surge of optimism I embraced since it compelled me to want to do something significant about my situation, which was to finally find a resolution for the pain I was feeling. There were five bottles neatly lined up in a row (so as not to spill), ranging from barely drunk to nearly empty. I must have looked ridiculous as I carried those bottles out to the lawn and then to the fence, where I ceremoniously dumped each one out over the top of it. Goodbye, Ketel One, you've gotten me through so much. Farewell, Smirnoff, boy, I must have been desperate to need you. Skyy, it was nice, but our time is up. Each of these bottles represented an opportunity for me to solve a problem from my past, and clearly, I'd allowed plenty of problems into my life.

The process of my alcohol dump was quite liberating for me this time, and I felt really great about it. A "that wasn't hard at all" type of great. Then I returned to the shed and cast my eyes on that mangled bike frame for another look and decided I would fix it. If possible, no one would ever see the evidence of its accident in time.

I grabbed a black bag from the corner of the shed and put the emptied bottles into it. I paused, and a wry smile surfaced. Then, panic; I quickly regretted dumping out my stash. What had I been thinking? In the past, I usually dumped it out on the ground when the mood hit me, only to swoop up the spilled contents with my hands before they were absorbed into the earth.

So many regrets consumed me, but I felt no need to dwell on them in the middle of my yard. It was time to return to the house. I was exhausted again and didn't want to fall over in my backyard. In addition to the cane in one hand, I now carried a garbage bag in the other. Just one pit stop to the garage to hide it until I could get to a public garbage can so my family wouldn't find it.

Once back in the house, I went into my bathroom and lifted up the cover to the tank. There was what I needed—a fifth of Smirnoff. It was time for a drink, my pathway to instant gratification in a world in which I felt so out of place.

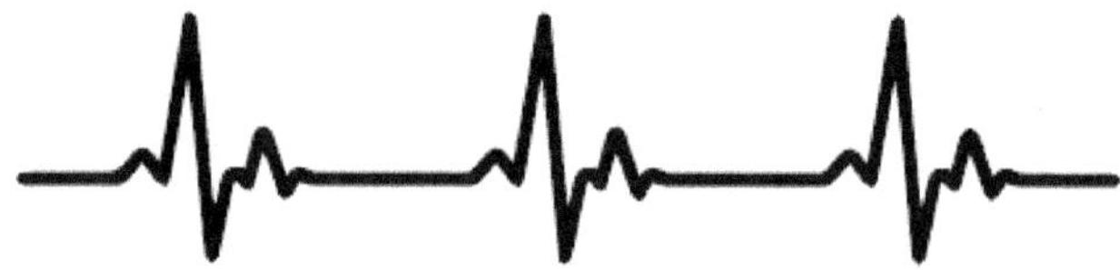

Mahatma Gandhi is known for simple sayings with profound meanings. "Action expresses priorities" is such a statement. Our words lose their meaning when our actions do not support what we are saying. As an alcoholic, how many times did this liquid take me astray from the words I spoke? Meaning, I'd say one thing and do another. It was far too many times, and it led to me being disengaged from the present moment. I was physically in a lot of places, but mentally, I was checked out. The most pressing thought of any moment may be how I could sneak away and take a quick drink. I used these thoughts as justifications; I'll take a swig and be more present then. The problem was that for much of my adult life, then never came. When my actions suffered practical consequences, the only solution I could ever snatch was a drink to calm down and refocus. Then, I would be emotionally available and engaged in family gatherings and other events. The only time it was easy for me to become relaxed was when I took a drink before a business outing to take the edge off and pry myself out of my shy shell so I could just feel normal…even for a moment. This logical theory can be a hurdle. When I was in recovery, it took a fair amount of time to finally accept that by adopting beliefs and behaviors that were more effective, I could stay away from those that were negative. Beliefs work because the right ones are disruptive to old ways by the nature of the way they work, which is good.

For so long, I'd built up the practice of expecting negative outcomes in my life despite living a life that was rather comfortable in the sense of a basic need. In hindsight, I have to consider that was part of the problem. I was never out of money. Being homeless was never a concern. I still had two loving parents and eight siblings who cared, although some had their own pressing issues at times

It can take a lot longer to get to your last resort when others can help you to some extent…at least until they have to quit on you for their own well-being and that of their circle of loved ones. (My ex-wife and sons understand this all too well.) And let's face it, in time, if you don't believe in yourself, others will follow suit. We all are the leaders of our lives, the ones who take the actions that bring us to where we are. Belief plays an immense role in a person's life and the value they place on themselves. Really, it is the lens by which everyone views their potential. For addicts, the bar they set for their beliefs just never seems to fuckin' workout. It's either too high or too low but never inspiring enough to achieve. For me, it was because I didn't know who I was on a level that was any deeper than that of son, husband, work peer, and so on. When I'd spend time alone, deep contemplative thoughts were often the furthest thing from my mind. It feels ironic when I recognize this today because, for much of my life, I've been more of an appeaser than a fighter—just "tell me what you want me to do and I'll do it" kind of thing.

It turns out, my complacency was no way to cope much less thrive; however, it was my biggest threat to my wellbeing. It was such a crazy mess of a personal message I relayed to the external world, which indicated I could find success in the commercial real estate world and work on complex concepts with ease. Yet, ask me what I was about, and you'd get a jumbled mess of a response because I could not answer what I did not know or sell myself to be someone I couldn't even pretend to be on occasion. Those were the types of answers that took more energy than I had to offer.

However, once the can of worms of curiosity about life is opened, be prepared for the flood of questions that will come for a visit. What do I believe spiritually? What is my value in this world? How is the worth of life determined? Is this what my life is really designed to be? When will the clarity I crave finally come? It's okay if it hits me in the head—I just want it to get here!

These are the types of questions that often cross my mind, sending me down a complex road of evaluation. Today, I embrace these moments and am certainly wiser about them. They used to be a source of suffering because I was not equipped to address such reflective thoughts. I felt like I had a sounder spiritual base when I was ten. That's a lot of years to fall further from the beliefs that define the life one chooses to participate in.

# 2 || The Lord in Lourdes

*A single event can awaken within us a stranger totally unknown to us. To live is to be slowly born.*
**—Antoine de Saint-Exupery**

A love of vacations, appreciation for adventures, and knowing you have a certain amount of privilege is awesome for anyone, and particularly a ten-year-old kid. Summers were so memorable, especially the ones I spent in France with Maman, who was a French native. These were joyful experiences, carefree and fantastic. Being the youngest child, with a twenty-year age gap between me and my oldest sibling, meant I got to enjoy these opportunities more times than my siblings perhaps did. I looked forward to it like a kid in a candy shop; the world was mine to explore, not just a single store.

When that time of year came around, I was always ready. It didn't take long either, just a backpack full of clothes and summer reading books for school, plus a bit of money to get me by. Papa would drop off the ones of us lucky enough to spend the summer in France at the airport and wish us farewell. We got the adventure and he remained behind to work. Papa is a very strong family man, having instilled the values of loyalty and hard work. Despite my challenges, I've always understood this to be the case.

Those carefree and happy days were blissful times, filled with adventures, reconnecting with old friends, and making new friends, too. For no reason other than a touch of pride and connecting me to an identity, I enjoyed having my dual citizenship between France and the US. I'd been given this at birth because it was important to my mother and the driving factor behind why I was fluent in both French and English. Maman always made us speak French with her and, as they say, when in France, do as the French do. Okay, that part is borrowed.

What captivated me most was the freedom I was given during these trips. Maman was loving and carefree, and that free-spirited and energetic nature benefited me with the opportunity to experience moments in time that would be unlikely to take place in today's world, including staying at a friend's seaside home in the fishing port of Loctudy, in Brittany. It was there I embarked on the train trip with my buddy and a youth group. Our destination was a place of miracles—the Grotto of Massabielle in the Sanctuary of Our Lady—in Lourdes, France.

This was a very Catholic destination for a kid who was raised in a fairly strict Catholic home. The traditions and rituals of Catholicism were always observed, and for me I embraced the entire process with my full, dedicated heart. Attending Mass with my parents was a given, and I gladly did all my "good" Catholic boy things and felt the love and grace of God upon me a lot. When I reflected on the good things my parents had in life, I naturally knew it was because of God's goodness and grace, plus their commitment to being their best selves possible in their respective roles. I figured life had worked out for my parents, and by following their guidance, it would work out wonderfully for me, too. Yes, that's the way a young mind thinks…it's good to know "what's in it for me."

Boarding the train was exciting and enticing—we'd be gone for a week. My friend's mom dropped us off at the train station in Quimper, and the adventure officially began. One chaperone who I barely remember and a group of ten(ish) year olds laughing and heading away for a holiday within my holiday was so cool. The fact it was parent-free was a blast to experience and likely fascinating to observe. Some off-color jokes, playing around, and adapting to the overall hierarchy of the group were all involved. But we all got along well, and it was an easy group of guys to not be silent with. Now, if I hadn't been able to speak French well, that could have been such a different headline: Shy guy gets railroaded by ten-year-old mob.

Whether the other guys had any strong connection to their faith was something I really had no idea about. It wasn't something we ever talked about, including my friend I was staying with. All I knew was I was about to visit a place of profound importance in the world of miracles within the Catholic faith. Seeing what it was all about was going to become real, not just a thought.

After the transfer in Paris to the highspeed rail system, it was only a matter of hours before we arrived in Lourdes, settled into where we were staying, and prepared for the next day's visit. If ever a night felt like a week, it was that night. My eagerness even drove my own self a bit wild.

With instructions on how to behave before we arrived at the Grotto of Massabielle, we stared at a humble entrance. For a moment, I thought it must be a joke. How could such a powerful place be so bland in its initial impression? Its simplicity was understated, but still, a sense of warmth and an invitation to enter could be sensed. Something about this basic moment stimulated a profoundly spiritual response within me, and I offered a quick thanks to God for what might come next. The

Grotto's shallow archway was rugged and jagged, which felt appropriate for those who enter to be healed because they are often at such a stage in their lives—desperate for the hope of a miracle to fix what is broken within them, physically or mentally. Being aware of this from my current perspective forces me to ponder if this could have been a place to help me heal from my addiction or at least help me become centered and focused on what it was about me that led to the label of an alcoholic.

This weathered-looking shrine quickly grew more like what I expected it to be with each step I took, including the splash of water that hit my leg. A reminder that the sacred Grotto sat on a spring and the ground below me was spongey. My eyes looked up to a statue of the Virgin Mary, and I saw that she was looking back down at me, making her seem alive as her eyes followed my movement. From the knowledge of the Grotto's history, which I'd read about before the trip, I knew I was at the spot where Saint Bernadette was said to have seen her apparitions. Having this statue of the Virgin Mary cast her loving gaze down at me felt like a miracle in itself.

As I traversed through this place of wonders, I felt the powerful nature of God everywhere. It was the sole focus of my attention, and outside distractions or random thoughts would have violated my having my best experience. My immersion was profound and inexplicable on a logical, age-ten level. Surrounding me were various stations of prayer and devotion. Candles flickered, with some guests deep in meditative prayer, silent but lips moving at a fervent pace; others agonized out their pleas for mercy in hopes God would hear them and answer their requests. There was no right or wrong approach to what anyone did, but a sense of connectivity with a Higher Power existed, demanding attention. The spring water gurgled lightly in the areas where it collected, a reminder of how fluid life can be. Such serenity has never been seen in my life prior to this day or since.

My senses teetered on being overwhelmed with the scent this Grotto had—it was so distinct. Earthy tones, melted wax, and intoxicating scents from fresh flowers were everywhere. They smelled so good together and in that moment, I felt everything was possible. Being simultaneously awe-inspired and tranquil in nature come to mind. I could see why the Grotto of Massabielle in the Sanctuary of Our Lady was a place of such significance, able to transform people of true faith and belief in an instant.

With my eyes wide open and absorbed in total curiosity, I made my way to a spot that bordered the Grotto where my eyes could lay sight on the evidence of miracles. Not ones just proven to be miracles by the Lourdes Medical Bureau, an institution within the Sanctuary charged with ensuring that claims of miracles are legitimate. All the testament to what has taken place at this Grotto felt like giant mountains hovering over me, forcing me to stare up in awe at them and absorb what it meant deeply and sincerely. Wheelchairs were abandoned, and those who were formerly reliant on them were free to walk out on their own accord. Crutches were strewn against the walls, no longer needed. There were also braces and all sorts of other devices that were meant to assist the afflicted, no longer required to be an aid to the one who'd entered the sacred grounds with them. And I got to observe all of this! For the balance of my week, I was assigned to assist the malades—those who were sick. With great care and compassion, my role was to cart them to the healing waters, Masses, and other services and help with their needs. Their looks of hope as they attempted to overcome their desperation touched my heart. At the end of the week, I knew life and my perspective of it would never be the same again. How could it be when I'd just witnessed firsthand the evidence of miracles unexplained?

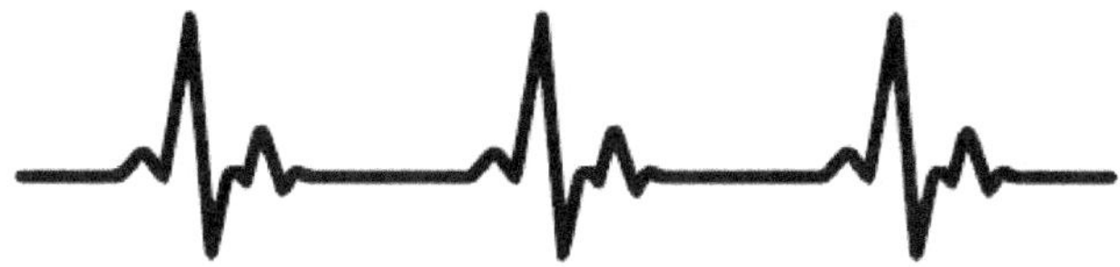

The words of Antoine de Saint-Exupery sum up what happened to be that day at the Grotto of Massabielle perfectly. It was a single event that woke up a part of me I didn't know I was craving, something unexplored before that moment. This sense of coming to life in an incredible way existed. As time passed by after that experience, a harsh truth hit home hard. It feels embarrassing that I was only ten when I had the single biggest encounter with the Lord of my life. I crave to come close to that same feeling again.

Maybe it was the all-encompassing love of God, or perhaps it was the visual evidence that He can heal, but it was extraordinary. Whenever I find myself caught in a daydream of this experience, I am drawn into reliving it as if it was happening in real-time. Recently, I even found a letter my dad (Papa) wrote me that summer, which said he felt I would go back to the Grotto of Massabielle in the Sanctuary of Our Lady. I pray he's right! Whether it is through the Catholic faith or another source, we all are being called to create a connection with a spiritual identity that will help us in life. My experiences at the Grotto of Massabielle remind me of this. Seeing these left-behind aids—both old and rusted as well as new and shiny—reminds me of how important hope and faith are in life. In my case, these were two powerful necessities that slowly faded from me without my full realization of it at the time. Somehow, over the years, I've lost sight of that, and it's probably a contributing factor to the isolation I felt in my life, convincing myself that alcohol could solve my self-perceived inadequacies.

I know miracles are a strangely contentious subject, and I feel this is the case for people who have never seen evidence of their existence. They say that faith is believing even when you can't see. For some personalities, this is a frustrating cliché; however, for others, it is a reminder that the most transformational experiences in our lives take place at the most unexpected times. There is no time to prepare, so one must be ready to receive it. It suits me well to embrace the miracle of sobriety in my life because it helps me to prepare for the hard work I have ahead of me to make amends and take the right steps to be good to myself. For an alcoholic, changes of heart that lead to new understandings are often considered to be a miracle recognized.

Not everybody embraces their spiritual nature in the same way I chose to. You don't have to do this; it's not a requirement. Regardless of where you turn to find solutions, comfort, solace, and joy, there are basic principles that are universally the same. We all desire inner peace, so we must act toward that, not against it. Understanding and meaning in the context of our lives is something we desire to obtain. Recognizing that we must offer the same compassion and empathy we wish to receive is important. All these phenomena take place through acknowledging a life connection to something greater than us; in this sense, there is no me against the world, only an unwillingness to connect to it. Referring to the tested and true Golden Rule helps me to remember this. When we do things to others as we want them to do to us, things become clearer. The problem with addiction is that we cannot do this because a symptom of the disease, beyond disappointing ourselves, is disappointing others. We are effectively receiving what we cast out, but it is not good, righteous, or joyful.

The Golden Rule becomes tarnished because what we give and receive is not healthy. Understanding this is strangely easy, which lends to confusion about how hard it is to adhere to at times. A pebble moving can crumble the mountain and create an earthquake of over-responsiveness and temptation. It is our spiritual connection that guides us to remain steadfast in this situation, so when we get lost in the shift and don't know how to connect to our spiritual side, we're left wondering what we should do.

# 3 || The One Strike Rule

*A man is worked upon by what he works on. He may carve out his circumstances, but his circumstances will carve him out as well.*

**—Frederick Douglass**

In the moments of our youth that define our paths in manners, large and small, we can change course. My defining moment happened in seventh grade. What a memorable, life-changing year it turned out to be. Parts of it I was all in on, such as challenging the rules and pressing my limits. It was enticement overload, seeing how far I could take my actions short of getting into trouble. Doing that excited me like it would most kids who would receive this chance. For me, all this was a way to get me out of my shy shell a bit, in part because I had some good friends to be comfortable around. So, it still blows my mind to this day how the one thing I had zero interest in was the start of a shift in my mindset, a fracture in the way I thought about myself and God's love for me.

My private Catholic school was divided into two parts—the K through 8th grade school and the high school. And if upperclassmen came and spoke to you, it was a big deal to the other kids, unless it was a sibling (and that didn't count). One day, I was standing outside, and a person was in the wrong spot at the right time for someone else. This guy approached me. "I was given some weed. Are you interested?" I'd never tried it before, and trying it wasn't something I'd even considered. This is evidence of what the mind thinks and the mouth mutters can be quite different. I said, "Yeah, sure," and had a brief battle of might with my nagging inner voice—the good guy—that had cautioned me to "just forget about it." A smart question would have been: Why is this guy giving me free weed? Well, it wasn't a day for smart questions. He told me I could find my free pot stash in the old bomb shelter on the school grounds. That was the real draw because every time a student went there, they got into trouble for it because it was unsafe. This was all it took to shut down the inner nag and put it on mute. I was going to make it there without any trouble.

I waited anxiously for the school day to end so I could get my freebie. Afterward, I made my way back to the lower campus, where my friends were, and started to hand out my score. We all talked about smoking it when we had a chance. Then we went home. As far as I was concerned, it was an experience that was over with, concluded.

Then, the little murmurs of discontent that spread around school indicated somebody was in trouble—big trouble, like an all-school bulletin that someone was heading down the fiery inferno and straight to hell. It turned out my bomb shelter connection did get busted trying to sell weed within days of me receiving my gift.

This guy turned from a fearless dealer to a seventh grader to a rat in a second flat. That's what a spirited, I have a point to prove: a nun principal can do to a kid. She can instill fear into the toughest of the tough, especially with the threat of a hickory stick to extract the details. In this case, she demanded to know everyone he'd approached about selling weed to. I don't know how many names he spat out because it didn't matter; what mattered was one of those names was mine. Without any opportunity to debate, discuss, or deliberate on the details, my parents were saddened to be called to a meeting with a dour principal who had just expelled me from that school. I was the last of nine How children to attend the school, the first one to be expelled. I hoped they didn't base the How legacy off me because it was embarrassing. I was pissed off about it at first, pouting about being busted mostly. Then, my heartfelt emotions would kick in, and I was filled with remorse about what my parents must be thinking. And most of all—I was angry with God, feeling completely abandoned by him.

This nun was supposedly a step closer to God on the scale due to her vocation, but she didn't portray the same God I had experienced a few years back at the Grotto. If only the former principal had still been there, she never would have expelled me with the same swift speed of an executioner. At the time, I was so adamant in this being the truth, and I blamed that principal for everything—so what if I had taken the action? The adult in the room had overreacted. Why didn't anyone tell me the rules were different now that there was a new principal in town? It was just one strike...and I was out.

Now, I faced a disgruntled Papa and a hurt Maman (her French disposition made this particularly dramatic for me, although she was just being her authentic self). Papa was a man who commanded respect, and I always wanted to deliver good on expectations. There has never been a point in my life where I didn't respect him. As for my beautiful mother, with her carefree nature and lovely disposition, her disappointment was a shock to my system and made me feel everything in my life was off-kilter like it couldn't get worse. I was unsteady, like a small boat on choppy waters. My parents' love for me was something I never doubted, so when this first run-in with the "law" happened, I was deeply impacted and left with horrible feelings about what a disappointment I must be.

For the small portion of the school year that remained, everything felt ridiculous. Despite the expulsion, I had a project I could complete on my own and hand in, and you'd better believe my parents made me do that. Ironically, it was on weed identification.

Then, in the final words to me from that cranky nun with authority, she hissed out words in her bitter tongue that were like nails in a coffin. Creased forehead, condemning gaze, and no love and compassion in her eyes, she said, "I hope there is a place for you in Heaven." That hit me hard! Those words about me probably not being able to make it to heaven haunt me to this day. They hurt all those years ago, yet I still go to Mass because I want to. Church provides a physical space and head space that always invites me in.

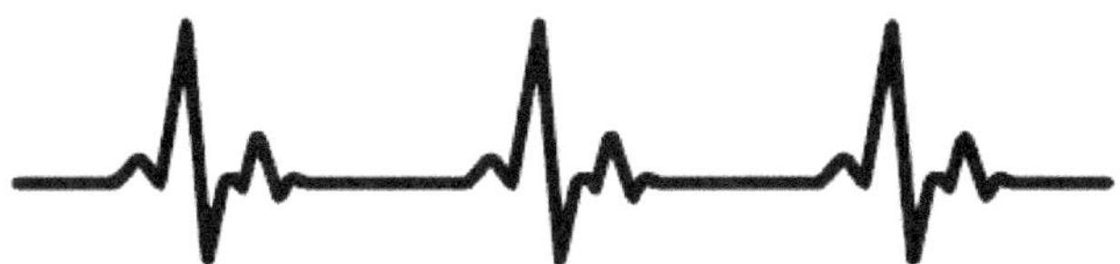

The words of Frederick Douglass really speak to the nature of our lives and the directions we, intentionally or unintentionally, take based on our actions. I tried to be associated with good and pleasing work in my young life, meeting expectations, being kind, and not ruffling a lot of feathers with stupid crap. However, dark forces were at work within me and gaining traction faster than I realized. I'd carved out a set of circumstances, clueless as to what they were setting me up for. Drinking was in its infancy, slowly leading me down a dark and twisted path. I had no clue what was ahead of me, but if you had asked me, I would have told you I was great; I had it covered. I meant it, too! After saying my farewell to my Catholic school, it was time to say hello to a new private school. I quickly saw a few familiar faces there—some of the other kids who had also been expelled from the marijuana shakedown. I just wanted to begin eighth grade with a new start, make some friends so I didn't feel so alone or awkward, and carry on in this new private school.

Have you ever heard the line "same mischief, new spot?" I hadn't heard this as a child, but I sure was living proof of it. My school life was surrounded by kids with financial resources who also had freedom and a knack for finding trouble. Parents were basically clueless as to what their kids did with all the money they were given. It sure wasn't spent at the arcade or movies all the time; it was used for more illicit purposes. Proof that being financially well-off is not always beneficial to a child. A parent can love them, trust them, and never think they'll take a turn down the road of drugs and alcohol. Ideally, they wouldn't. It's this illusion of an ideal that leads to numerous unideal situations and circumstances.

I was a sucker for this trap, justifying it with my good grades and staying out of trouble. This was an upgraded version of me. I'd gone from sneaking weed out of a bomb shelter to purchasing illicit drugs on weekends quite easily—as it wasn't hard to get— and I wanted to experiment with these temptations. I would occasionally drop acid and go to whatever world the tiny little tab led me toward. Or do a little crank, and then I will be ready to conquer my universe. And if we went into downtown San Francisco on the bus and ended up on Haight Street, the risk of possibly being robbed when we were seeking our weekend fix was a risk we were willing to take. This seedy world was much less violent back then, a little give and take between those of us with resources and those who sold us our fares. Today, the intensity of life between those who have and those who don't are much more toxic, I think. But let's face it, a drug user is a drug user, mentally altered, whether they are in high-end Atherton or on shady Haight Street. The big difference is the support and resources behind a person to help clean up their mess if they find themselves in a situation.

So, drugs became a part of my culture by default. My friends used them more than I did, but I participated. What I never did was invite the problem into my own house. It felt unnecessary when my friends had parents who weren't as active and engaged in their kids' activities or were from broken homes. More things slipped through the cracks when I was away from home, which made me feel I had everything under control.

On these weekend hiatuses with friends, alcohol also crept its way into the party. This enticed me the most because I felt different when that liquid slithered down my throat; it liberated me, and I was able to come out of my shell a bit and relax. Would I have been more cautious then if I had today's knowledge of what my life has brought me? Honestly, I don't think so because I just needed to feel more normal and less awkward, and that was the easiest way to make this alteration happen. Who'd ever think a kid in eighth grade would meet the same criteria as a "functioning addict," a statement I despise because some part of me was dysfunctional, even though I had no clues as to what or why I felt this way. So in my stage of maturity, I thought, fuck it, and just went with the flow. I was smart enough to hide my deviant behaviors from my parents. I just needed to be respectful and kind to them, be ready for Sunday Mass, plus keep good grades. This guy wasn't about to be humiliated by the walk of intense fear that came with each step down the hall toward Papa's home office with a report card that was less than stellar.

There were also times when staying off my parents' radar wasn't easy because they are smart and observant—just like many parents who know when their child is trying to fool them. But I was diligent in doing my best to hide what they would find unpleasing, which came with side effects. Constant feelings of anxiety and stress were compartmentalized in me so I could maintain my constant vigilance not to let some clue slip. It was a pressure I imposed on myself because they didn't know what I was on the cusp of becoming.

My weekends charged me up for the week, and my week depleted me just in time for the weekend. By suppressing those emotions that might betray me and show what I was really feeling, I simultaneously fed the underlying issues that contributed to my addiction. This all led to a question I've often pondered: How can you determine what you are feeding your mind when you can't state, specifically, what the problem may be? This really comes down to how you define it. For example, some people think shit is bad, while others find it to be a great fertilizer. It's all about how your perspective processes what you're fed. One thing alcohol was for me was a social lubricant from eighth grade up until my sobriety. I have found people don't necessarily understand shyness and its impact. I don't easily warm up to people and tend to keep smaller social circles. This doesn't fit the outward appearance of when you're conducting business because a shy person can be quite outgoing with a topic they are confident about. Work is that topic for me, so it really illuminates on me strangely when personal friendships stem from work situations. This makes me a Jekyll and Hyde in this scenario; I find myself feeding off the alcohol in order to toss out my social inhibitions and feel functional around others. It has often felt like an unachievable dream to be accepted as I am, stimulant free. When these feelings are present, they feel unsurmountable.

My social lubricant was the only thing that helped me to relax and let my guard down for most of my adult years. I was able to relax at work outings, be there for my wife when we first met, and not feel like the world around me viewed me as a misfit. The problem was, I wasn't a misfit; I was ill-equipped to get along in a world that didn't rely on a buzz to function.

Alcohol became my medicine to solve whatever ailed me internally—my mysterious disease of a life of dis-ease. It helped me out in a way but didn't solve all my challenges. One major problem had to do with my relationship with God, not other people.

Unwavering faith and belief in God had always been a given and was uncontested. As a child, I found the Catholic faith to be one that instilled fear to obey God into people all too often. The situation in Lourdes at the Grotto was a rare and precious gift to me but hardly one that would give me the fortitude I'd need for a lifetime of challenges. Look how easily a person can crumble away from something as important as faith. It took just a single line from a snarly-faced nun to confirm I probably would not have a place in Heaven. Religion is not perfect, just as we are not perfect. It seems we do need religion in our life, though, because it is a way to start meaningful conversations with the One we deem to be our Higher Power.

# 4 || Into the Wild

*Knowing others is intelligence; knowing yourself is true wisdom.*
**—Lao Tzu**

I have to hand it to Papa; when he wants something done, he gets it done. For me, this meant uprooting me from Atherton, my home base for my life thus far. The new destination was Pebble Beach, so I could attend the same college preparatory boarding school he had gone to. At the time, this was a move I was vehemently against. It made no sense to move because all my friends were in Atherton, and I loved it there. And with a boarding school came a slew of new rules and a sense of confinement, basically a loss of freedom. It was like a prison, and I was not eager to be taken in. In the end, Papa won, and I was Pebble Beach bound to prepare me for my future. Oh boy!

This school was on a beautiful campus, as you might imagine, richly adorned buildings filled with old artifacts and beautiful architecture. Young adults from many rich countries and diverse cultures went there; these were bright, eager, and prepared youth, ready to go the distance for the futures they craved.

Despite the rigorous academic schedule of a college prep school, I tended to do quite well in that manner, using the occasional vodka snack to unwind. The dorm life, however, wasn't great because I still opposed the loss of freedom and the separation from my friends. Thankfully, my parents started transitioning to Pebble Beach to live, which meant I could stay with them from my second year onward. Sophomore year came, and with it, the buzz about the big event for that year picked up—it was the highly anticipated wilderness expedition. You could elect to do this challenge, but it was a great idea to participate for college application reasons if nothing else. This expedition was a test to see how a person fared in the world beyond what could be learned in textbooks and such, a man versus nature event that was high school-approved. We all felt invincible before it began. We assumed it would put us in league with Lewis & Clark, Grizzley Adams, and all the tough guys who faced the wilderness and won. In our minds, we were kin with these pioneers of the past. In reality, the situation was totally different. Sure, we had to survive, but it was with a group of sophomore guys and girls. Still, it was kind of a big deal, and the one teacher and senior who were our group leaders would be the ones to guide us if anything happened to go awry. We—okay, at least me—thought, what could possibly go wrong? This college prep activity was meant to showcase our resilience, not demonstrate ineptness.

There was a small group of us on this trip, and we were required to train before participating. Training for the wilderness cannot be offset by training at home or in the gym—not even comparable—and we quickly discovered this.

Not long into the trek into Los Padres National Forest, which is Big Sur backcountry, we realized how unequal the preparation was. Some of the girls struggled with sore feet, small nicks and scratches, and a general disdain for an outdoor environment with lots of bugs and too few amenities. This wasn't just a girl thing; a few of the guys had challenges of their own with the beautiful backcountry. It was kicking their asses, and for many, it was their first adventure out into the wilderness. I'd been fly fishing in remote places before, but this did feel different; it wasn't me and the water. It was us immersed in the wild. The challenges were made worse by those who had mindsets that taunted them about being so inadequately prepared.

Next came the lesson in fate. You see, fate has a wicked way of slapping a person when they're feeling most vulnerable—like a solid smack in the face. The unexpected change of weather from intense cold to freezing rain to eventually snow was evidence enough that our resume stacking trek was taking an intense and unfavorable turn. Like good students, we looked to our leaders for help. What I saw was a bunch of uncertain faces staring back at our group with doubt in their eyes. They acted casual and in control, which was a deception that perhaps worked on some but not me. I had some experience in deceiving and wasn't all that gullible, so... I assessed these leaders and saw textbook uncertainty. There was no way I was going to leave my well-being to them. Someone had to take charge, and I stepped up to be that person. My shyness was now more of a reserved personality, and I could step up and be a leader in a time of need.

Today, getting out of such a mess would be considerably less problematic. In the 1996 world I was in, we had no cell phones, satellite phones, or GPS to offer us anything helpful. We did have topography maps, which were hard to read and assess in the blizzard that swirled around in the howling winds. Our first step was to set up a ridge line and camp to get us through the situation. Starting a fire was no easy task because none of us was Bear Grylls-level prepared. I'd get it done, though, and I did.

Whether I was the true leader during that time or not didn't matter; kids were starting to turn to me, and the anointed leaders consulted with me, too. I got the camp ready, meals prepared, people fed, and even comforted a few girls who were cold by putting my arm around them... or was it them keeping me warm? In hindsight, I muse at how typical thoughts for a high school guy didn't tempt me more—it wasn't that type of a situation. I was driven by a desire to be victorious and return us to safety and warmth.

Seeing uncertainty and fear in others sparked me to step up. When I sensed the chance for true peril, it compelled me to act fast. I had to keep people prepared and unified. The challenge came when I tried to instill this same level of assurance in a kid who was memorable for the wrong reasons. He was scared and inexperienced, wreaking of urine from pissing his pants.

At one point, I grabbed the topography map and gave it a scan. I wasn't a pro, but I knew enough to hopefully get us by. It was a bear of a task because the damn thing didn't reflect the environment. Snow had skewed how everything looked. There was a road somewhere nearby, and after one miserable night, our goal was to make it to that road the next day. When our feet finally felt the solid road below them, it was a small victory won.

This road might as well have been paved in gold. It was the best sign we'd had for help in two days. Then, glory be, a vehicle started coming up the road.

Our arms were waving frantically to get the driver to stop, and he did. Despite the situation, I had to smile because he was what I'd expect in the Big Sur area—a Zen Buddhist hippie kind of guy, living deep in the Los Padres National Forest, on his way to his homestead with some supplies. He took us all back to his cabin in the wilderness. Thankfully, he had a phone and let us use it so we could call for a ride back to the school. The cabin was an experience within the experience. Glad for shelter, I was not able to unsee what surrounded me. This guy had a fine collection of stuffed taxidermy, with his obvious preference being for mountain lions. They were staring down at me from the walls; they were stalking me from their stacked spots on the sides of the cabin. These preserved dead animals' eyes followed me everywhere I paced, and I couldn't shake it. It wasn't at all as pleasant as the watchful eye of the Virgin Mary in the Grotto. The word bizarre comes to mind, but it seems like an utter disservice to the shrine of death this Buddhist kept.

When the headlights grew brighter, and we saw a vehicle winding down the guarded and tight driveway toward the house, we were elated. We thanked our temporary host and loaded up into the vehicle. Body was pressed against body, and you didn't have to be sitting next to the "urinator" to feel like you were starting to absorb his smell. This poor guy must have been so distraught, but I never asked, which is a failure in effective leadership. You worry about the team more than your role.

Finally, we were back to Pebble Beach—earlier than expected and worse for wear. When I got to the duplex, no one was home, and it was locked. Maman and Papa were back in Atherton for a visit.

By this point, ready to sunset the wilderness adventure, I found a stick and busted out a window and crawled through it, groaning the second I was inside. I was cold, and it contrasted with the sweat, dirt, and grime of my body. Plus, I was so hungry. I wanted to restore and replenish myself physically quite badly. But I chose a shower first, then followed by a steaming cup of clam chowder and a healthy brandy snifter, before crash-landing in my bed to get the sleep I craved more than the alcohol. Adventure over, mission achieved. My reward was my bed—my divine, comfortable, and awaiting bed.

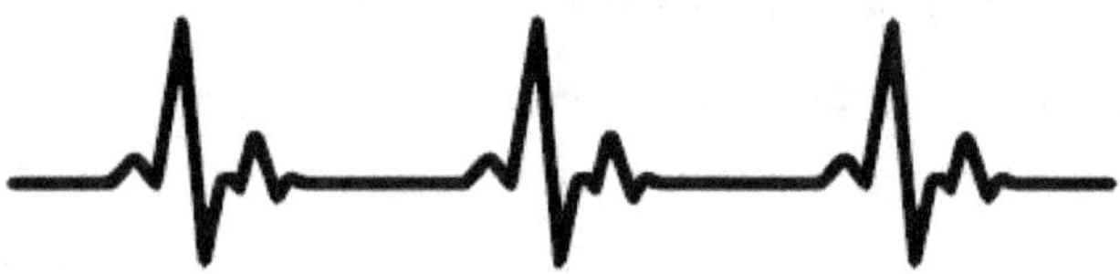

With a fair amount of frequency, I have recalled this experience in my life. The words of Lao Tzu, legendary in the Art of War, seemed fitting. He said that when you know others, it is considered intelligence, but knowing yourself is where true wisdom lies. Despite it being a challenging situation, it made me feel alive. I wasn't sure how I had the confidence to step up and be a leader for the other kids. After all, I had no more experience with freezing weather and snow in a rugged environment than they did. Something just compelled me to be the one who took action. It felt so good and provided me with unintentional positive vibes to carry me for a bit of time. I felt like I understood my purpose better, but was this really the case? There was no self-reflection afterward to attain true wisdom. I could have followed a "what to do if you get stuck in the wilderness book" and reached the same conclusion.

Since then, I've pondered how a show of leadership in a rough situation turned into a weakness I would someday use against myself. What I know is that when we create a sense of importance about ourselves and our actions to receive a psychological boost, we receive feelings of purpose and value. It would be unnatural not to want to embrace these more often, I think. At the time, what we don't realize is we are susceptible to these acts of confident leadership turning away from us. Suddenly, we are fearful of what it means to have others rely on us, and if we falter even a bit, we lose more of the confidence we gained. Without warning, life becomes skewed, and we are lost in an abyss of inadequacy.

These struggles are painful, even if no one else knows we are having them. When you aren't a person who sounds off on concerns to others, it doesn't help. Living in an image-conscious world, we have all been tough on ourselves and had others who were tough on us, too. Not necessarily bad-intentioned but definitely not understanding of how what works for others doesn't necessarily work for us. I would have gladly been that successful fluke story, solving my every problem by relying on others. However, what was slowly happening in my life that made me vulnerable to addiction wasn't fully recognized by me. I kind of remember thinking that if I didn't fail at things, people would like me more. It made sense to me, but the impact of what that could lead to was as foreign to me at the time as getting a bad grade—it was inconceivable.

Over the years, my anxiety about being everything to everyone else became all-consuming. It was paralyzing, and without my consent, it began to plant seeds that would grow a plethora of negative coping mechanisms. For the life of me, I cannot understand why I was prone to these feelings of inadequacy when my entire life had been mostly fantastic. I would even say that it was still fucking great at this point. So many great things were a part of my youth. My heart swelled with joy when I went surfing during my senior year on the Monterey Peninsula; it was an epic regular activity. Its picturesqueness and beauty are world-class awesome. Waking up to drive there in my truck and meet my friend before calculus class was an ideal way to start a day. How lucky was I? In hindsight, I get it, but at the time, this was just the flow of my life. I was a sandy—a flip-flops and chinos sort of guy—crushing it at school and spending my lunch hours tossing a frisbee in the quad. There are no do-overs, and I am not sure I want one or would accept one, but those were fantastic days. Everything went well for me for a long time. I graduated from school with 120 great kids in my class; we all got along and were ready to pave our futures in the most vivid hues and glorious manners possible. These were days filled with big dreams and optimism for our outcomes.

Now, when I look at that, it's kind of like that Springsteen song Glory Days; it hurts to feel I am not the guy with all those opportunities any longer. Today is harder, but it is also better because I know what I have to do to keep my best chances at sobriety. And to this day, I tend to future-trip when I am starting to get anxious. I realize the signs and how to slow things down during these unproductive, and frankly a bit scary, moments. Dwelling on the past to reconnect with who I was then is neither possible nor healthy for me. Yet, focusing on the negative aspects of a situation, then or now, is easy to do because negativity takes a harder line in our thoughts than positivity. I know that now, which helps. Glory be, I've finally come to the realization it serves no purpose for me to ruminate on past mistakes because they lead to shame and guilt, two feelings unhelpful for anyone and possibly detrimental to a recovering addict. I know I have guilt from the past, and my mistakes are mine to own, but they are not moral failings as much as regretful happenings. They do not define who I am as a person or my truly authentic self. If we could all take to heart this profound truth, everyone would be better off, regardless of what their recovery battle is.

When Elizabeth Gilbert penned To repeat this, dwelling on the past serves no purpose for your present and future. We've all had experiences with trauma. Everyone has days when they don't feel great about themselves. Look out if you get bored because you never know what you may turn to, so you can mix your life up a bit. There will always be somebody you feel is better than you, so stop comparing yourself to them. All these thoughts are ones I remind myself of frequently because they keep me grounded in the type of recovery I desire to have in my life.

# 5 || Keeping the Secret of My Sauce

*First you take a drink, then the drink takes a drink, then the drink takes you.*
**—F. Scott Fitzgerald, The Great Gatsby**

Access to many things that bring me happiness has never been a problem. Unfortunately, these were just things, nothing of any personal substance, and I was prone to taking a great deal for granted. When I reflect upon this expectation I had in life, I gravitate toward being a country club member. The bells, whistles, and elite golf courses that come with these types of memberships were mine to enjoy. No place outshone the club in Pebble Beach, which my family was a member of. It wasn't me that made it possible to be there; it was Papa. My life had never known a time when I didn't get to experience a world of luxury. In my younger days, this posh life provided by my family was my identity, and I loved it, especially whenever it allowed me to play golf, a game I loved and consistently tried to master.

By this time, my parents had sold the house in Atherton and were living in Pebble Beach. On weekends, Papa and I would play golf and oftentimes run into one or two of my older brothers who were in town. They'd join us for a round. What was most memorable about these days was that through golf, my family and I had something to bond over. This "guy's guy" world was one I could navigate better than other areas of life...it involved personal pressure and expectations more than being what others felt I should be. If you have a certain perception of the country club elite, you're absolutely correct. No shorts or jeans allowed— proper golf attire and what people refer to as "business casual" were dictated by the dress code. I was a rebel for a time with my shoulder-length hair; it didn't really pass muster, and I sensed the keen gaze of disapproving eyes on me. Because of this, my shoulder-length hair didn't last too long.

Golf days were always some of the best. Once the cart approached the tee, it was focus on, distractions out. This was competition time, not only against whoever was in the group but the course itself. These courses were not easy and tested a player to the hilt. Teeing up, adrenaline rushing, remaining calm and focused to maximize your swing. All of this was important to the game and something I wanted to master. I guess you could say my drive came from more than my driver; it came from my determination to win if at all possible.

When the round was over, the routine was always the same. We'd head over to the men's grill to have some drinks and play some games. Such fond memories remind me that although I was younger than my brothers and everyone else in the men's grill, I was still one of them. I was genuinely happy and at ease with the world around me. My goal was to always be as grown up as my father and siblings, not the age I was. That was the key to making our bond work. I had no clue whether it was good for me, but I never thought about it much because it didn't bother me.

As we set up this country club picture from my experiences, minors having drinks was never a concern within the parameters of the club. Not a single word of caution or Papa telling me I couldn't drink come to mind. The staff never questioned me, probably because I was always ordering drinks for the table. No big deal, they probably thought. No big deal, I definitely thought. A few drinks was a normal thing; it's not like I was getting blitzed or out of control. Plus, I carried a solid 4.0 GPA, so there couldn't be anything wrong with me. I held life together quite well. No temptations existed that might have suggested I was teetering on the edge, on the brink of spiraling out of control.

In a world where alcohol is the norm, which was my world, it is problematic for a reserved guy to not be someone who indulges on occasion. This is what I felt to be true, therefore I operated as if it were the truth. These touches with alcohol were essential for loosening the muscles for the big game, a little something I call swing lube. I was convinced that golf and a few drinks were my key to success. For as silly as this may sound today, at that time, it was logical. Just like a glass of wine with dinner was expected, swing lube helped me get my game ramped up. Eventually, those few drinks after a round of golf turned into a pregame party, followed by an on-the-course party and after-party. But darn, I was the most refined partier you ever saw. There was nothing to be concerned about, right?

If you've ever wondered why golfers like to have a few drinks, there is an interesting aspect behind it. A drink can calm the nerves and hone the focus. Add a caddy to the mix, and you can have a decent round of golf. My belief in my process was steadfast because it justified my competitive nature. I always wanted to have the best score, and that meant playing boldly. Naturally, bold is hardly a word that fits me, but with a few drinks, watch out. My inhibitions dissipated like a storm cloud, and the risk-taker side of me took over. I can honestly say I loved that guy. He could do anything. When I had to redefine my relationship with this alter ego, I learned about hard work and obstacles again. It was strange and difficult, yet enticing. Like any alcoholic

I've crossed paths with, I believed my relationship with alcohol was beneficial and helped me be a better man for a long while. It was no different than popping an aspirin for a headache and feeling on top of the world again a short time later. Problems went away, and worries subsided. I felt in control and headed for a glorious destiny; so alive and much older than I was, all thanks to the social lubricant that aided me in growing my confidence.

Let me go back to the games at the men's grill at the club. These were key to my feeling integrated and bonded with my dad and brothers. These moments also helped me learn how to socialize with people of affluence like I'd have to do for work in time, refining my skills and making me feel like a natural in these types of environments. The games we played were basically older guy games. I didn't know anyone my age using logic, math, and calculating strategies to play hearts, gin rummy, liar's dice, or dominoes. I was a great thinker who had learned how to hang out with the big dogs, so to speak. I talked a great game, played a great game, and had the look of a winner. What was missing from my self-proclaimed mastermind was the impact of being comfortable with people who were older than me more than my own age. We couldn't compare life experiences, but with games, we were on an equal playing field. And I liked being treated like an adult. I didn't have to be my age and be the young fool so many guys could be. What I failed to see was that most times, young fools grow up and become these same guys I'd skipped the line to join.

Perhaps the ugliest thing that occurred from this lifestyle was the feeling I got. I was entitled. I was a man in charge of my day and my future, deserving everything I received. Little did I understand how, later in life, I often did get what I deserved. The caveat was it was never what I wanted. It never occurred to me that I functioned differently than others; I was in the dark about the relationship I was taking on with alcohol. No one close to me noticed it either. My favorite golf buddies wouldn't have taught me that because they all enjoyed their libations too.

By the time my senior year of high school ended, I had this confidence I was set to face the world—and it would embrace me as I was in whatever I chose to do. I ended up going to school in Boston. I went there blind, sight unseen. What a bad idea! College prep had prepared me well educationally but the environment was so different. I was a fish out of water, gasping for air and longing to be back home. It might as well have been on the other side of the world. California was all I'd known for schools, so to end up there in an environment where nothing was familiar—no courtyards for gathering or even my small circle of friends—made me lonely from the get-go, and I drank a bit more. The things we do in the spirit of coping can become quite toxic. It didn't take long to see I was longing to return to California and all its perks, which meant a transfer to Santa Clara University, a Jesuit school with an approach to education I understood.

Upon returning to California, my drinking was minimal once again. The world was mine for the taking, from my first serious girlfriend to the way I was approaching life. If life were a triangle, it would be school, girlfriend, and golf. I was independent and healthy, really at my best, with any desires to drink kept in check for the next few years. Who needed it? I didn't have time because my "triangle" occupied my entire bandwidth. However, it entered into my days during finals because they were taxing on my psyche, and I still loved alcohol in secret. The problem was that for each moment of struggle I began to drink so I could re-ground and refocus—it worked for golf, why not for school? Today, depending on where you stand, my graduation was either successful or a failure. I obsessed about if I was good enough, smart enough, and efficient enough with what I did. I still felt like I'd failed because something in me knew I didn't do my best and I wasn't the best either. This self-judgement was bad for me but I hid it from the world. If you'd ask my family and peers they'd share I graduated with great success.

San Francisco called my name upon graduation, sans 2002. My first job was ideal for me because it was in commercial real estate and investment, which was a perfect industry for an alcoholic in the making. Booze was everywhere, as most accomplishments and celebrations included it. It took one glass of the glorious liquid slithering down my throat to calm the nerves, prepare for the round of golf or business meetings, and enter my destination with what I would have called swagger at the time. Today, a wry smile crosses my face when I reflect on this. Actually, I can't believe I pulled it off. How I felt inside compared to how I looked outwardly was such a contrast. My insides were always twisted, leaving me uncalm and untranquil.

During this time, I began expanding my horizons and joined several golf and social clubs, just for variety. Of course, there was the Pebble Beach club, but I also joined The Olympic Club and had access to several other prominent clubs. A guy with options and without limits—watch out world! This false sense of security served my needs. If I made a small mistake my next move would be extra special. Almost a "hole in one" at times. Or a big commercial deal at others. Others felt I handled the stress masterfully. What would they have thought if they saw my love of the secret sauce to my success—the alcohol—as the key to me presenting my all-pro image?

The alcohol was a band-aid to my discontent. Every time something felt wrong or off, whether I consciously realized it or not, a drink would help me gain the poise to manage the situation. It was the fix I craved and it kicked the butt of any adversity that came my way. Until it didn't… until I stopped functioning at a high level… until I finally had to admit my life had some negative shit going on in it that I would eventually need to have a reckoning with. With all those "until" ideations being shoved into the deepest corners of my mind, I chose to believe I could control what I did. I felt like a genius being able to fool myself as I drifted through my increasingly unmanageable life!

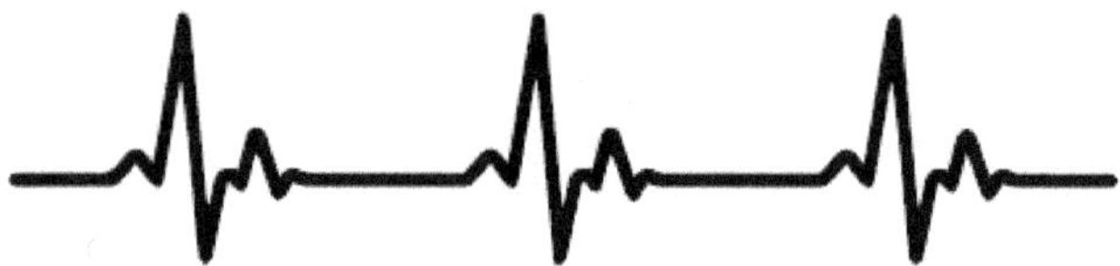

If I had been alive when F. Scott Fitzgerald wrote how we take a drink first, then the drink takes a drink, and finally, the drink takes us, I would have sworn he'd been a fly on the wall of my life. I wonder if every person with alcoholic tendencies goes through this. I would imagine the answer is yes. But why?

In my situation, alcohol helped me function socially. It was the ticket out of timidness and reserved nature. It provided me the only gateway I could find to be able to carry on a good conversation with people, sometimes those I knew and definitely those I had just met. This meant I felt alcohol was necessary, almost a condition really, for new relationships, whether business or personal. It also had a powerfully perceived side benefit at the time—it helped me feel better about those unknown mental trappings which tagged my subconscious. In hindsight, it is fascinating to explore what all my reasons were for choosing a drink to solve the problem. What I do know is this is utterly illogical today, but it was natural back then and effective until it stopped working the way I wanted it to. This is a common situation for many addicts, I feel.

I am uncertain if someone is born with alcoholic tendencies or if they unfold as a person makes the choices that define their life's direction. In my case, alcohol was always present in my environment, and there may be a genetic predisposition to it in my family. Maman always found it natural for the entire family to have a glass of wine with dinner. It wasn't a big deal and I wasn't a young kid drinking a lot. It was just part of our meal experience. Seems "normal," right? Especially if you are familiar with European culture and customs.

Papa and my brothers drank a bit more. Papa liked to relax with a mixed drink when he got home from work. Or, we'd play golf, then drink. It was fun and we all bonded over it. Does that mean that we all had a drinking problem back then? I don't think so, although I know I have a sister in recovery and siblings with alcoholic tendencies, plus a dad who drinks but is able to function. And really, does it matter what I think about this? Alcoholism impacts others but it is how you create a relationship with it and your recovery that matters most. All these questions about alcohol that I still ponder show its impactful nature on life, even during recovery. Truthfully, I have to learn to let some of this go because I will never be fully satisfied by any answer I produce. More likely than not, one answered question leads to a new question, and so on, and wondering these things for the remainder of my days doesn't resonate with a fulfilled life, which I will live. Acknowledging my problem is important, and understanding what to do should temptation arise is necessary, but understanding how this process works for others is practically impossible. I have understanding and empathy but solutions are so individualized that they are greater than my capacity or desire to solve them. Yet, if someone is willing to listen, I'll do my best to try and help.

What I loved about my hay day of drinking was its magical ability to make me feel problem-free and less awkward, at least for a bit. This gave me the freedom to escape social anxiety, have more natural interactions with others, and feel a connection to the world around me. Behind the scenes, these benefits were tarnished with a sense of me being superficial, too fearful to be my authentic self, along with all my faults. It really underscored the importance of how our genuine connections require vulnerability to be just as we are. If you don't feel vulnerable you are probably hiding something important. Maybe from yourself, maybe from others. Its impact surfaces when you realize what that hidden detail is, and it may leave you feeling either liberated or sad, maybe both.

Philosophically speaking, when we are unauthentic, we cannot reach a place of self-actualization. This is why it is impossible for addicts or anyone who shoves themselves into a false narrative to answer, "Who are you?" A square peg will never fit perfectly into a circle, no matter how hard it tries to convince you it can.

I'm drawn to gaining a better understanding of a concept called a Hedonic Treadmill that is used with substance abuse at times. With this concept, it is suggested that people who live to chase happiness tend not to be happier at all. They actually become worse and experience a decreased state of happiness. Life isn't all about being happy and that expectation is part of what places stress and burdens on a vulnerable person's psyche.

When I came to grips with how others did not expect me to be happy all the time it screamed a harsh truth at me: that was my expectation for my life, not theirs. Happiness is not a constant but a fleeting moment, so you better know who you are and what you're up against for the rest of the time. Take a lemon, for example; it can sting the heck out of your eye if a squirt of juice gets in it. This same lemon can also quench your thirst in that perfect glass of lemonade. It's your perspective for the moment.

I've said it a lot, alcohol was the answer, not the problem. When we desire something, it's often mistaken as the solution when we are truly craving something deeper, something more meaningful. Learning to recognize and manage desires was an important part of gaining an understanding of who I was and what I really longed for.

And it wasn't alcohol; it was a sense of purpose. I find this more daily as I recover physically and mentally from the low points that alcohol invited into my life. Do you know what it's like to be so alone in a crowded room? This is a feeling that doesn't subside even when you are loved, and if you don't love yourself how can others love you in the way they desire to? So, I return to the one thing I do understand: the lessons a person endures in the journey to getting to know themselves. These are a beautiful part of the tragedy of addiction; events worthy and deserving of self-compassion. I think of the verse of walking a mile in someone's shoes. There's no better way to get a grasp on a situation. It comes back to being vulnerable and letting people into your darkness so they can know you when the light returns. We all have a place in this world that needs us to be as we are and contribute to a greater purpose.

# 6 || My Social Clock Was Ticking

*Marriage is a strange combination of dream and reality, and we spend our lives as couples trying to negotiate that divide.*
**—Elizabeth Gilbert**

When I asked for her hand in marriage she had no idea of the journey her "yes" answer would take her on. And frankly, I had no clue either. I understood my parents had longevity on their side, a devoted marriage going nearly fifty years strong. Any effort it took was mostly hidden from me but admiration for what they'd done existed. What they had was what I wanted, and that meant my life as a married man should start the same way—a French Catholic wedding in Paris, just like Maman and Papa had. It felt like a wonderful way to show my parents how much I valued them and my future wife, how much I valued her.

The setting of Paris, with its rich history and strong Catholic tradition enticed me. Maybe I'd even be able to reconnect with God in the same way I had all those years ago, still missing the feelings of that moment. I knew it wasn't a give-me when it came to getting married in Paris. It wouldn't be as easy as it seemed it should be to take our vows there due to several reasons. For one, the cultures were different. Two, clearly there were communication barriers to overcome, more for my future wife than me. However, the seriousness of our vows and the love we had for the city existed, as we both loved everything about Paris and French customs. Plus, Catholics only marry one time—and forever—so it should be special and spiritually significant. That's what the sacrament of marriage was meant to be for someone devout to the faith. For all these reasons, the City of Lights was calling us. We had one chance to convince the French Catholic church we should be married there. I was so nervous about the conversation I was about to have and gaining favor with the church. My nerves were intense; sneaking away to drink a bit to calm me down and open my heart for the conversations became a logical preparatory step. My mind longed for loquacious French words from the heart to spur on the response I desired most—a yes to the request. I could speak French fluently and my future wife could not, so I was the voice for both of us when we met with the Pastor at his church, Église St. Roch, a church whose first stone was laid back in 1653 by Louis XIV. As someone who loves history, this church had everything to offer, from architectural marvels to religious significance and of course, a beautiful wedding.

The Pastor was an impressive man. His office was in a church with more grandeur than anything I'd ever seen before. Tall pillars and arches were laden with gilded artwork, stained glass windows, statues, and beautiful depictions of Jesus that connected you to God in an almost chilling, yet profound way. The Pastor's office was considerably more humble yet beautiful with its rich mahogany accents. We walked down a corridor with marble floors, each step we took alerting anyone in earshot as to where we were. Finally, we were in the room that might determine where we could be married.

Wise and kind eyes looked at the two of us, a look of discernment laced with concern on the Pastor's face. This was a man who never had to demand respect but provided a presence that imposed it be given. Small talk is always a powerful way to start big conversations. I didn't want to dive right in so I complimented the building and asked questions about it, to which he responded kindly. However, he was not a tour guide, and this was a serious task, so he started the conversation with a short prayer, followed by his initial thoughts. Before long, we were immersed in a conversation about the universality of love and the diversity of cultural expressions of faith. We listened to each other, and I absorbed his every word, completely stimulated by the conversation. It was an undeniably meaningful exchange of ideas and I followed his lead, enveloped in what he said and not interested in trying to cut down his plethora of reasons why we shouldn't be married in that church in France. If it were to work out, my future wife would have to seek an annulment, as she had been married once before.

The Pastor really brought out a spiritual side to me that had been previously unexplored, piquing my interest when he shared insights on the transcendent nature of love, something that existed outside of the constricts of boundaries, nationalities, and language. We discussed how Catholic weddings are a sacred union that transcends cultural differences and unites two souls in a bond of love and commitment under God's umbrella—the three strings of man, wife, and God which make the strongest cord. The priest saw firsthand that I was well-studied in the rituals and customs of the Catholic church, although I am not a Bible reader per se. I just felt so connected to it all and the philosophical principles he shared, and with each statement, I wanted the marriage to take place in Paris with increasing urgency. A major point of emphasis was the importance of faith, prayer, and community in the journey of marriage. The church was meant to serve as a spiritual anchor for couples seeking to build a life together. We both agreed on these points and perspectives, yet I instinctually knew I remained in an uphill climb with the pastor to receive his blessing for us. We kept conversing back and forth, and it was obvious that I was steadfast in my resolve. Finally, a concession and some progress were made. We received the Pastor's blessing to marry at Église St. Roche but with a caveat. The marriage would need to be officiated by an American Priest, Pere Brien McCarthy.

So, off we went to meet with Pere Brien McCarthy at his parish Église de la Madeleine.

Much of the same conversation took place, although this time, it was between three people, not two. Having grown up in an Italian Catholic New York family, my wife-to-be was well familiar with the traditions and expectations in the House of God. After much discussion and reflection, the priest agreed to officiate the French Catholic wedding, and we were married on May 29, 2010, with close friends and family in attendance.

After the ceremony, we hosted a reception at the Hôtel de Crillon in Marie Antoinette's piano recital room. It was beautiful and grand, a magical spot to see, an ideal place to begin life as a married couple. I was captivated by my bride and the moment.

The day I got married remains one of the most incredible of my life; it was a time when I felt a connection to God and His design for my life in a powerful way. Despite life not turning out the way I felt it would that day, it is still a day to behold forever.

I'll forevermore be grateful for this experience, as it spotlighted the importance of perseverance, open-mindedness, and respect for different cultural traditions. What I bore witness to reinforced my belief in the power of love and how our differences do not have to be our divide. I learned how the universal values which bind us together as human beings provides us opportunities to experience how the power of love can provide the strength to get through obstacles stronger in faith and closer to God.

This story was the start of our marriage and it makes me feel better than the start of our dating life did. Single and living in San Francisco, I went out a lot. The Lion's Pub was a hotspot because they had killer greyhounds (fresh squeezed grapefruit juice and vodka), plus a lot of beautiful lady patrons. People went there looking for other people, making it a primo pickup spot, or meet your future spouse spot.

I was sitting at the bar and at least ten greyhounds deep into the night (I told you they were tasty). My buddy looked over to me and said he'd be right back. I had no idea I was getting the Irish goodbye until I had to admit he'd ditched me and was gone, leaving me at the bar solo. Not ready to go home and not wanting to be alone, I called a buddy from high school and he joined me. He started to drink and I continued on when two gals walked in, and we started to chat them up.

These girls were very pretty and had a few libations in them to make the conversation flow more easily. Maybe it was our wit, or perhaps the greyhound drinks, but they were interested too. One of these ladies batted her eyelashes at me and I sure didn't mind. Our talk was casual and flirtatious but it was already late. We had to go. Upon saying our farewells, I mentioned where we were going to be for a New Year's Eve party the following week, and then we left. It was out of sight, out of mind. It had been casual enough that we didn't exchange any info either, so it was interesting to see these ladies show up at the club we were at on New Year's Eve. This was the start of our history in the making.

This woman ended up being like a lot of my friends, kind of mature and someone who would hold me up to a higher level of personal accountability. It was logical because I learned she was a few years older than me. I used to laugh about that probably more than I should have!

Then I got zapped by some new information. Her email address had a name that was different than what she'd told me her name was. Detective Derrick was now on alert.

"How come you have a different last name on your email?" It turned out she had been married before, and it startled me. She was only about thirty and I had no idea how someone could take the journey to marriage—especially a Catholic—and already be divorced. It did not compute. I had some concerns and decided it was best to proceed with caution.

We lived near each other, which made it easy to date her in a big city.

The two of us had a lot of fun, which I always appreciated.

Her best friend was full-out dating my friend, which added to the fun.

So, we ended up getting more serious for these reasons, as well as our growing fondness for each other. It all made good enough sense that the prior marriage shifted from startling to a caution flag to being compartmentalized into a tidy little pocket hidden from my conscious thoughts. Out of sight, out of mind! I never even asked too much about this guy because it felt so strange to do so—and I'm sure she didn't mind my hesitation either.

When her friend and my buddy got engaged, it kind of shifted the dynamics. I was his best man at their wedding and murmurs of my next steps started to surface. Were they expecting we would be next? It was a topic I didn't eagerly discuss because I just didn't know what to think or what to do. Yet, I was almost thirty and according to all those social norms I was susceptible to, I should be getting engaged and married.

And I pressured myself right into getting engaged. It wasn't a matter of having no love for her and wanting to avoid starting a potentially beautiful life together that got to me.

The real challenge was that a part of me wasn't ready, so if I were going to get married, it would have all these criteria attached to it. That's when my beautiful story in Paris began. I'd put my heart and head in the right space for my forever commitment but I also knew I was cautious to not let the future wife see me drink as much as I did. And there was no doubt in that glorious hindsight which has kicked me in the ass so much my behind has a dent that my high-end Vodka habit clouded my judgment at times. I had the "Keep up with the Joneses" disease, feeling that by doing what others did I would blend in and my struggles would not surface. I was in control, not under the influence.

After the wedding, we dove headfirst into all those things married couples do. We bought a condo together and started a family. She kept her successful job and I kept mine. She stayed type A and I remained laid back. We were opposites attracted to each other who also diverged enough to never be truly aligned. And this is where our fairytale wedding began to tarnish—and not just with small challenges like what many marriages face.

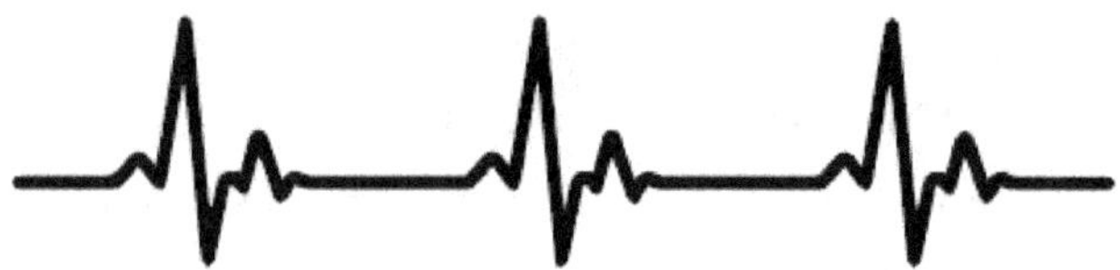

When Elizabeth Gilbert penned that marriage was a strange combination of dream and reality, it took me to a place where I could fondly reflect on the wonderful side of marriage. Unfortunately, the second part of this quote brings me to some of the reasons for the demise of my marriage. I find that the more we negotiate that which divides us the more we tend to lose ourselves, which never bodes well, especially in the arena of secret keeping. This leads to the cycles of debate about relationships and what is an acceptable amount of give and take to make it work while not turning yourself miserable to appease someone else. Even the best-intentioned people are susceptible to this.

From where I stand, every person—whether they feel they are or are not—is impacted by the result of this, which is called normative behavior. In order for society to get along we all have to conform to some type of societal standard or norm. For example, we wonder why someone who is of marrying age doesn't have a spouse, or at least date someone. We start to think of what may be wrong with them. It's a cruel injustice to cast this heavy thought upon us. Differences exist between all of us and our circumstances vary. Then there is the well-known Hierarchy of Needs by Abraham Maslow, which states "belonging is fundamental human motivation, and conforming to societal norms is a way to ensure inclusion within a group or society." If it were only as easy as that statement makes you feel it should be. In my life, I've never placed a super high value on being like everyone else—consciously that is. In my subconscious, I still carried those same expectations of certain societal norms, such as marriage and family. I am prone to the chronological timetable of expectations being achieved for me, including graduating, entering the workforce, getting married, having children, and eventually retiring.

Yet, I have broken that chain in my life. I have children, I was married, and my abuse of alcohol has led to me needing to rethink everything. It's scary sometimes and it would be easier to not look these obvious concerns in the eye. You can only avert what needs your attention for so long though. And that competitive side of me never wants to be behind on anything, even if it is not a good thing for me.

Being a laid-back and chill guy has always been my forte. I feel comfortable in this space. However, I remain vulnerable to the same challenges as those Type A driving personalities. I do want to embrace a level of success, and that can come at a price, like my internal peace. The way I spent many years responding to my feelings of inadequacy and failure of what I perceive others want of me was to retreat to the bottle, and maybe go fly fishing or golfing for some fresh air. For all these reasons, conforming is a word I am uncomfortable with to the point where I view it more negatively than positively. Whether it is forcing a way to feel accepted into a group of people or just relying on others' intelligence to form my opinions, it just doesn't work for me. If this works well for you, you hold a magical secret that should be shared.

What does work well for me today is the pursuit of my authentic voice. It's okay that I'm not perfect because I never claimed to be the unachievable in the first place. But I perceived others expected this from me, including my wife. I set our relationship off on the wrong foot from the start by not opening up to who I really was as much as trying to be who she needed me to be. And I failed! I still struggle with that failure at times because it still feels so negative, despite my personal growth.

That's why I take life one day at a time to learn, to grow, and to reconnect with a world in which I learn about myself through the adventures I have. I try not to care who is an upward social comparison—someone perceived to be better off—or who is a downward social comparison—someone worse off. My esteem and sense of worth cannot be bracketed by others and my perception of them. Knowing this makes a positive impact on my life, plus helps me be less judgmental. Who are we to judge others?

# 7 || The Dark Spot in the Joy

*Alcohol is a perfect solvent: it dissolves marriages, families, and careers. The one thing it never solves is problems.*
**—Unknown**

The dynamics of the family I grew up in meant the man—the husband and father—was the head of the family. Naturally, I assumed the same outcome would take place in my life. I didn't mind because I was raised well, and following in my parent's footsteps didn't feel like it would have any negatives. Never would I have imagined I'd be butting heads with myself and my wife when it came to this topic. My wife never told me I wasn't the head of our household, yet clearly, I was a head case with more issues than I'd let on. Being laid back meant surrendering just to keep the peace and avoid an argument. I truly do appreciate my wife never claiming she was in charge. I've also come to acknowledge it was me who didn't feel confident to adhere to the more traditional role I thought I should be tied to in my married life. One day this all hit home, hard.

I'd been working at my job in San Francisco for eleven mostly amazing years. I loved every aspect of it. Negotiating deals. The way the industry worked. It never hurt that I could incorporate a good golf game into the business plan either, socializing and doing business over a few drinks. My days hadn't changed much, aside from not letting my wife know how much I was drinking, which was increasingly more.

My wife was no stranger to hard work. Intelligence, a desire to demonstrate her value, and feeling she could manage it all were driving forces for her. Her work in corporate finance suited her well, resulting in many great opportunities. How she managed to hold it all together and get things done was a bit incredulous, to be frank, especially when she was pregnant with our first child. Long productive days, plus taking care of herself worked for her in a way it might not for others.

Remembering these qualities about her has forced me to take that trip back in time. Just a glimmer of the happiness that led to our marriage in the first place is what I long to feel once again. I still struggle to fully process how a committed, nearly three-year's courtship could feel so different than the first day of marriage onward. What I can say is the "I dos" turned the tide of my mindset and shit got real then.

Between a fast pregnancy, finding a new place to live, and all the pressures of this new life I'd decided to pursue, I was not prepared, at least not in the way I thought I should be. It was a shit ton of pressure. I wanted to become a father at the right time but all I felt was uncertainty and worry. I had no clue how to evaluate if I was ready but the choice was made for me when my wife became pregnant.

These maddening fears consumed me constantly, like a flesh-eating disease. Dire thoughts of my own inadequacy looped on repeat. Playing out "what if" scenarios blurred the lines of reality with my perceptions of what it should be. To me, my wife was completely on top of everything she needed to be, always prepared. Then there was me, the great pretender, making it seem like all was well even though I had increasingly more miserable thoughts. It was depressing to see how I lacked in so many areas. This was my perspective, so no one other than me could change it. But damn, that took work that was tough to handle because it was more self-reflective than I dared venture into. The fact about how tough this type of meaningful self-evaluation would have eluded me.

Still, a symphony of discourse continued to mount in me. Some days would be amazing but it was seldom that it were multiple days in a row. If I didn't get in my own way with some thought I felt was important, I craved a drink for perspective. If it was time for one of those serious discussions about where we needed to do better, be better, or achieve more, a drink helped me focus on what I always perceived as something I was doing wrong. My wife had every right to state her concerns, which often had to do with my lack of emotional accessibility, just as I had every right to not disclose to her how much trouble I sensed I was heading toward. It was a wicked loop that never solved a problem or moved us forward, and this was practically right from the get-go. I understood she had her own concerns to process, and it just so happened these variations took us on separate journeys within the same household. Have you ever heard of that working well for a unified marriage? It really doesn't, at least not for the type of marriage I wanted to be in. I wasn't mentally equipped to become vulnerable to my wife so we could grow together.

This sounds apocalyptic—complete gloom and doom—and you may well be wondering what the heck I was thinking. Like all these toxic relationships, regardless of casting blame or aspersions, we had so many wonderful times too. We both loved to travel and any new spot could become an enticing adventure. The journeys to New York to visit her family and go crabbing were so fun. They often included these massive traditional Italian feasts, such as the Feast of the Seven Fishes. Truly an incredible feat to pull off and marvelous to enjoy. There were trips to Baker Beach in San Francisco that were fun adventures. Swimming in the pool in the backyard during the summer, sipping on limoncello to quench our thirst and get a reprieve from the heat. Before kids, we took romantic weekend getaways to the vineyards. Plus there was a lot of laughter at times, which was always good for my soul, just as people say it is.

Those adventurous trips for two were now mostly nonexistent from my life, which felt like a grinding task to me, slowly shrinking me down to a shell of a person. It got to the point where life was more real than I was with myself. Before I knew it, the day came when my first child was to be born. I was so excited for this moment, and to hold my son for the first time. It was such a special time of reflection when I looked at his beautiful little self and promised I'd always be there for him, to be a papa like mine was with me, involved in his life and excited to bond with him, make a connection that mattered, you know? After he was born, it was hard to leave my son and wife at the hospital, but they had to stay a couple of days, leaving me to time go home to an empty house with my many thoughts.

By the time I got home from the hospital that first night, my emotional exhaustion from the big day started to catch up to me. Gratitude was there but I grew tired so fast, a physically exhausted body with a mind that wouldn't shut down. There was no longer a baby growing in my wife's belly but a presence in this world that relied on his parents to be at our best—not just Mom but both of us. As excited as I was to begin the journey, I was a bit freaked out. I sat down and had a couple of drinks. To celebrate my son, I told myself. It set me up for some self-therapy, convincing myself I would be fine. It was common to be nervous, I said. I'll get over it, I claimed. Yet the murmurs of doubt kept rolling into my mind with all the momentum thoughts could muster. Are you sure? And no, I was not!

Then life carried on with my wife and new son.

One thing that subsided my fatherhood fears was the shifts in my workplace. They replaced those concerns and gave me a new plate of worries. I no longer loved my job and had become more of an asset manager compared to a hunter of properties; it sure was lackluster to the preferred traveling around and not being confined to a space. With everything else happening, I hadn't fully realized how my shift in responsibilities would become so ill-received. Plus, another round of news—a second child was on the way.

I kept plugging along and we sold the condo we'd purchased, deciding to rent a house in a suburban setting. The city was no place for a growing family and we wanted our kids to have space to roam, not a condo to be confined in. This transition to a more suburban setting became a bright neon light blinding me, forcing me to admit how drastically my life had changed. It was ridiculous to think life could stay the same for many reasons. I was in my thirties, for one. My responsibilities were to a growing family, not just myself. Sadly, I was so focused on myself that others' needs became secondary or a fleeting thought I had in passing but chose to ignore. Word got to me about an exciting opportunity to work with a new company and I thought it might be the fresh start I needed. For me, the equation became: growing a family plus a new job equals a new me. It was worth a try. If only the equation was as easy to follow in life as it was to read. My wife kept moving fully ahead with her work, not letting anything stop her. She appeared to be the Energizer Bunny. Always going, never showing me if she was slowing. Only now can I see how it was probably harder on her than she ever shared. And if she had spoken her heart to me it was unlikely I would have changed my course of destruction. It was well underway.

In a very short period of time we had moved three times, making for boxes, babies, and a whole lot of stress!

There was this dark spot in my joy. Life was coming at me hard and heavy from every angle. At first, it was great to get that new job opportunity. It came along with a new title and more responsibilities, plus a prestigious golf club membership. (If you're thinking, oh no, you're correct.) Between buying real estate, managing others in my office, and my personal issues that were catching fire, it felt like my head was underwater and my ears clogged. The world around me was talking but I couldn't quite get what it was saying.

I'd work, go to the club for some drinks, then decide it was time to face the home life. I did what I felt gave me my best chance of making it through the muddled mess I was facing. The order of importance of my life's activities showed just how far I'd fallen. Work came first, and my health and personal life second. By the time my second son was born, I was undisputably a man digressing from his best self, unable to fool anyone. For every big acquisition I worked on, my company was glad I'd "exceeded expectations." It was a platitude that got me by and I just kept grinding it out and trying to exceed their expectations. The doubts I had were exacerbated by some of my peers just being assholes—they were not nice. I was bothered by this, yet I managed to push it aside and kept working my tail off to produce results. My efforts might have been a bit too effective because the whole organization got stretched thin, making it feel less organized and efficient, and like the powerhouse player its reputation had sold it to be.

Time spent traveling for work and being away from home was more common than time at home. It was good for hiding my increased desire for drinks, just to cope at times or wind down. Every single thing became one unresolved stress spot after another. As a sea of pressure washed over me and crashed at me from all angles, I felt like I was starting to drown. To make matters worse, my role with this new business was about to revert to what it had been at the old one—that of an asset manager. The company had grown the portfolio more than expected so fast. I didn't want to do that, or anything else. And for the first time, I just wanted to be at home.

Also for the first time ever, I talked to my wife about what I was feeling and going through. The words were direct and forthright, a rarity for me: "I just can't do this job anymore." She saw how miserable I was with it and understood how it was affecting me. She tried to help but we thought on such different levels, making her good intentions ones which didn't quite compute with me. Never being one to view my problems and find a logical solution by doing A, B, and C to resolve them, her strategy was met with a verbal "makes sense" from me, followed by...nothing, absolutely no change. But I did get what I think I truly wanted at that time, which was to quit my job and become a stay-at-home Papa. Who needed the not-so-great nanny? I could do all those things; it would be an ideal opportunity for me to bond with my sons and my wife, trying something new to rejuvenate my energy. Our agreement was to try it out for a six month trial basis, then take it from there. My wife had some incredible work opportunities on the horizon as well, and my being present at home more would also be a sign of support for her chances to achieve her goals. Yes, I sincerely sold myself this new "ideal," which was a sincere intention made by a breaking man.

I really loved being at home with my sons. Keeping the house and taking care of my boys was the easy part. It gave me so much more freedom than what I had felt I had before. And what did a guy like me do with my freedom? I tended to drink—I'd sneak a sip here and there, hiding a fifth in a place no one could find it. With the taste of freedom I'd been given, I started to drink myself out of any sense of freedom at all. Forget about keeping up with my responsibilities.

Things started not to get done and life became a code red emergency. Well, I'd managed to turn a six-month recharge into six years—with a few rehab attempts—so I had that going for me. (This would be a good time to understand sarcasm because you just read it.)

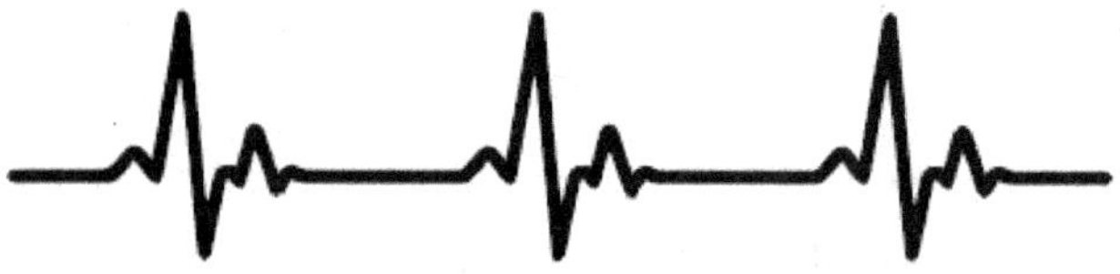

Alcohol is the perfect solvent if you want bad things to happen to you. It does so much more damage when it becomes a problem than what you'd ever have to face otherwise. Besides dissolving marriages, families, and careers, all things I have experienced, by the way, mask the reality of life behind the hazy fog of an unclear mind and definitely unclear intentions. You're never at your best and can only hope you can avoid others seeing you at your worst. It's miserable.

My life had so many things happening within it that would not have been a challenge if I weren't doing my darndest to hide my growing addiction. Believe it or not, I hid it somewhat well for a long while until it was just so obvious that people knew about it. Papa never said anything to me about it but in time, Maman would express her concern and beg for me to get the help I so desperately needed. My siblings did too. However, that was their thoughts, and I wasn't ready to get help from all involved, so I blew off their love and kept my stubbornness. Most of us understand stubbornness, but how do we justify acting this way even when we see how we'd benefit if we'd just heed others' advice or warnings? It's a common response from alcoholics, and from my experiences, it is one that is often acknowledged in hindsight. You may say, "Better late than never," but I say, "Finally!"

When it comes to alcohol and addiction and our unpredictable responses to our problems, you can turn to existential philosophers, such as Jean-Paul Sartre for example, and find a great deal of content regarding how the root source of the problem is a lack of authenticity. I know my lack of authenticity has been a major theme in what I've shared with you thus far. When you make decisions that do not align with your own values, choosing to conform to societal expectations, you can be tossed into the throes of addiction faster than a spark can ignite a fire. Life events play such a critical role in this, and if I'd fully recognized the impact of this when I was first married, I could have been a greater man by being honest about my struggles. Instead, I chose to conceal, don't feel. This type of coping didn't solve a thing but brought on plenty of new burdens in my life. What I needed was to gain some tenacity and show a bit of stoicism and control. It wouldn't have taken much effort in these areas to show I struggled but did care.

On one hand, I was great at focusing on what was within my control, such as work, but horrible at accepting what was out of my control, such as alcohol. If you resonate with this struggle you just need to realize you are capable, so long as you are ready to take on the work. It's hard and there can be just as many "fuck it days" as fulfilled days, especially at the earliest stages of your sobriety quest. And when you fall, you fall hard too, sometimes drinking more and heavier than ever before. For those of us (yes, me) with multiple rehab stints, this is obvious. Each failure at rehab leads to a more major setback than anything you ever thought you could endure. It can always get worse for an addict.

Do you align your identity with any specific narrative? For so long, I did. My identity was everything around me mostly and not at all about how I viewed myself. This was a big mistake and if you happened to fall into this same trap, I feel for you because it sucks. And when you feel your best friend and source of comfort is the bottle you know something is wrong, even if you have zero idea how to handle it. You just know... Have you ever heard the term hedonist? It is one that many alcoholics resonate with even if they don't know how to define it. I've finally grasped what this means, and it has helped me gain a valuable perspective I would like to share with you: Pleasure is viewed as the highest good, so when alcohol makes you feel good, you assume it will last. However, it doesn't last because, in time, reality catches up with you, and the more you rely on alcohol, the less you rely on resolving your issues before they feel insurmountable. The first step I took to a lasting recovery was to explore what aspects of my life made it possible for me to cover up my addiction, or live in denial. I tried it all and it always worked for a period of time. It wasn't until I admitted alcohol could never solve my problems that I was able to start exploring my heart and the way I thought about life.

# 8 || All For the Father

*Just as a candle cannot burn without fire, men cannot live without a spiritual life.*

**—Buddha**

My struggles grew more intense and I was like a kite that had been disconnected from the string that guided it back in. When I was alert, the focus was filled with good attention to my sons—alert and responsive to their wellbeing. More than anything else, I wanted to be certain that no parts of my multiple life failures reached them. They didn't deserve it. This was an unachievable hope, something else on my wish list that wasn't done. Love is not enough, although it sounds lovely. Life has logistical needs that surpass this, such as a sober father to drive them around for one example.

One thing I wanted for my sons was more sentimental than necessary. Since Maman was French born, I had received dual citizenship with both the US and France by blood. It had always felt so special, despite it being mostly a piece of paper. Maybe it was this little feeling of being special that made me want to ensure my sons felt the same way. It could be the start of a new tradition with my sons—one that was personally important and brought with it a way to bond. It would be fantastic if I could take my sons on their first trip to France, a beautiful country with amazing memories for me. The same opportunity of dual citizenship was also given to my wife to make it a real family affair. For her, the process was more complicated. She never did go through the hoops or complete the paperwork; it doesn't seem too presumptuous to guess this was never a pressing issue for her or a big deal. Just something novel more than necessary. I understand it well enough, but at the time, it sort of felt like a rejection from her of something special to me. It festered inside of me, remaining internalized by my unwillingness to address anything that bothered me.

The most important legacies I wanted to hand down to my sons were those involving a spiritual foundation. Catholicism was the best choice since my wife and I were Catholic, therefore our sons were born into this religion. We followed all the early life rituals, such as baptism. My sons receiving this sacrament was important to us, plus expected by our families. It was something you did, without question. It's quite strange to think about in hindsight because baptism is about committing your life to God, and that is a matter quite personal in nature. So, in actuality, a baptism where the one being baptized states they want to demonstrate their commitment to God is what is enduring. All children are protected under God's love...so the kids were covered. It was me that wanted to make sure I was covering my spiritual bases with them. Anything to help.

One aspiration I had for my children was they would find a path to their personal prosperity that wasn't laced with a driving force—albeit still mostly unknown—that a drink had more potential to heal than a connection with God. It would have been nothing short of heartless and cruel for me to feel my precious sons could end up making the same choices I did—the easier route that glossed over challenges and left me in a situation where no one could rely on me. I abused how I relied on people too, starting to tell those little white lies to cover my tracks. It is surreal to love your children so much, yet be pulled away from a loving connection with them because it's easier to do that than not take a drink. Life was becoming quite lonely for me and it impacted my sons in ways they still can't express to me.

Everything was starting to implode, from the life I was living to the one I wanted to give my sons. I felt fake. Moments with God in His house were beneficial, however, His power to heal and change my heart lost their sizzle the second I exited that glorious building devoted to His teachings. I am not sure if those actions were the reason I defined myself as more of an imposter over time than an authentic follower, but the irony of it was never lost on me. The result was always the same—I felt the guilt and shame of not measuring up to what was expected of me if I were a "good" Catholic, which aligned with being a devout father and family man.

My wife went along with these rituals because she also felt a sense of honor to adhere to what was expected of her as a mother; they were the right thing to do. However, she was not someone who went to church except on certain religious holidays. Other than that, she didn't mesh with that aspect of her faith at all. Since she didn't go to service, I didn't go either.

Yes, that's an excuse but we always seemed to have something else planned, and it was something I was expected to be a part of. I kind of chuckle, knowing it was good she wanted me there but simultaneously curious if she just was keeping an eye on me more than anything else. I was okay with both because I did want to strengthen my family ties, despite my struggles, and her looking out for me held off the inevitable day's end conclusion of self-medicating with alcohol. So, to put it into perspective. To be a good husband, I had to become a good father, and to be a good father, I needed to have the ultimate Father in my life. Still, I was a Catholic in name only during this time. One day, I said something important. "I have a drinking problem. I need help." More than I actually wanted to get help by stating this, I knew I needed to appease my wife in some way to show I was trying to become better. It was understood that I was an alcoholic and she wanted to understand my perspective better. Why did I drink? How could she help? Why can't you just stop? What was going on with me? At this point, the clues of my disease were never the alcohol itself, but the impact that the alcohol had. Shakes at times, not feeling good, having to sneak away to get a taste of the "hair of the dog that bit me." It was embarrassing and still, I was not ready to change. For the sake of our sons and family, I made my first failed attempt at rehab. Afterward, my wife and I began some counseling sessions with a substance abuse counselor.

Those meetings were surreal. I started out by trying to express what was happening, but the second I was challenged, I grew quiet, and then there was no getting me to talk about it. In time, every session became more of a Q&A between my wife and the counselor. I wanted her to have a stronger grasp and understanding of my struggles but I didn't feel the need to be a part of it. She was smart and could learn what she wanted to on her own. I still had little commitment to any authentic participation in the process. I was doing it for everyone else. That was me, the great appeaser and I appeased my wife until even she had to admit it wasn't worth her time to go. My wife and I were getting nowhere, hostilities were mounting, and the underlying current of tension toward each other was easily detected. In a way, this attempt at therapy resulted in a negative outcome for the boys because no matter how award-winning we felt like our "everything is fine" acting was, the tension was so close to the surface that it was sensed. Some may call BS on this statement but it feels true. Kids are so smart and they can sense adult tensions better than adults at times. Just another reason why I love my sons so much and want to be better for them. How wanting to be better for someone can go so wrong. I used to not know, but today, I get it—I just couldn't get out of my own head to better understand their needs. I have used up all my credit for trying but rest assured, I haven't given up on trying. These two guys mean the world to me.

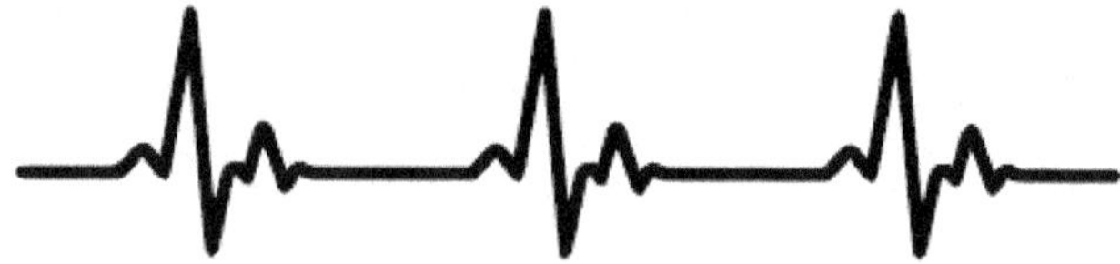

The tranquility Buddha's wisdom provides are nuggets of wisdom I can count on. I feel the positive force of statements like the quote at the beginning of this chapter, which indicates the importance of people having a spiritual life. If we don't acknowledge the presence of anything greater than us, we take the burden of life on all alone and are isolated from others during our times of joy too. I've been at both ends of this and don't recommend it; it's miserable. In my life, I call this greater source God and embrace the solace I find in the Catholic church. This is special to me, a home for my thoughts and heart. Whatever it is you find that helps you to expand your awareness and makes you feel less alone is something I humbly hope you embrace. The problem is that when you live life like an imposter, you really have no chance of successfully navigating the self-love process. You have to go about deprogramming yourself from being what everyone else expects so you can begin the arduous yet enlightening process of exploring who you are—what makes your heart beat and brings clarity to your world. My wife expected me to be a good father so I strived to be one. Only, we weren't fully aligned with this, and in time, she was hurting so bad, and that carried over into how my boys viewed me, too. This is when our toxicity for each other really ramped up.

It was far too long since I'd recalled the reasons I fell in love with this woman, the mother of my children, and through recovery, I've been able to reconnect with those moments. Not all of them promoted actual love, such as trips to wineries but they were fun times filled with good conversations. We carried the weight of the world like it was a helium-filled balloon—light and carefree, embracing our chance for love. That helium eventually became a led zeppelin, and something had to give, rather than someone, and it was me. I became dysfunctional and it was like a shoreline slowly receding. You don't know immediately but in time, you see the damage that's been done.

I had given up on myself, which was basically me waving the white flag of surrender to the best parts of my life. Through all of this, although it wasn't as strong as it could be, it was my connection to my faith that really helped me find the courage to hold on one more day. Through the church, I think there are so many benefits that a person can put in their spiritual arsenal, helping them be better equipped for battling their demons, whether they are alcohol or something else they know is not serving their best possible life well. For one, the church provides a community where you belong. I'm not saying I ever have been or ever will be someone who hangs around at church after the service to take advantage of the social aspects of the community. However, when there are others who are sitting in those pews around me, I know their focus is on God and solving their problems. We all have problems, and I find this to be a good thing, a reminder of our humanness. No one person has everything under control to their personal definition of perfection. If the wisdom of this type of message can be imbibed on my sons, it will hopefully save them grief, helping them choose the path that doesn't lead to self-loathing and destruction.

The moral framework of the church is also beneficial. Sure, churches are full of sinners and run by them because none of us are the Father, we are the children. And just like I desire for my sons to be redeemed, I know they will sin and that as their father, my devotion to them is endless. And with the Father, there is endless love for them as well as expectations to strive for morality. What I feel most in my heart and hope my intentions and actions will transfer to my sons is this message: I will always love you even when I don't love the things you may choose to do. You didn't ask to have a papa with the struggles I have had. Yet, you do have a Father who can help you through everything, and He is someone your papa relies on too.

# 9 || Going From Great to Late

*At the end of the day, the most overwhelming key to a child's success is the positive involvement of parents.*
**—Jane D. Hull**

When life lacks authenticity, it can leave a person feeling they are an easy sell; after all, they lack an understanding of their convictions. One can convince themselves of how their false hopes and expectations are the real deal. Acting in such a way is like selling snake oil to yourself, and doing it successfully. All you know is you crave being better and want the chance to make a change.

I always understood it is hard work to take care of young children and a household. Logically, it's easy to grasp. Not surprisingly, the logic goes by the wayside of addiction quite effortlessly. You get desperate and the more you try to handle life with a modicum of grace, the more small fibs "accidentally" fly out of your mouth and the more likely it is for mishaps to occur. Attempts to cover them up work for a period of time but not in the long run. Lies and secrets catch up to you and this never happens on a convenient day.

My sons are authentic little beings and they instinctually knew what their days should entail. When they wanted to play, which was most of the time, I eagerly satisfied their whims to be a pirate, police officer, or whatever they needed me to be. There was always one caveat to their requests: "Just give Papa a second." And in that fast second, I retreated into the kitchen, grabbing the first travel-sized vodka I could get my hands on, and drank it down quickly so I didn't get busted. I even had a lie ready if one of my sons would have seen me. "I just have a small headache; that's my medicine." Thankfully that never happened. Then I'd go and be whatever my sons needed me to be, selling myself that I was present and, oftentimes, pretending I was sober. If my destination were a graphic, I would have been in a huge downward plummet heading toward ground zero.

There were days when I had tremors so bad it seemed certain my sons noticed, despite their tender ages. Making my youngest son's bottle up was an event in itself at times. My body would have twitches and shakes like I was standing on the fault line of an 8.0 earthquake. It was like threading a needle with someone jerking your arm around. The best solution was always to take the edge off with a snippet, or two, or more.

At times, my wife would come home and I had gotten exactly zero done with the tasks I volunteered to complete. This sounds like a dick move, and I admit, it is. The lack of remembering what I said I'd do, coupled with being the star and sole attendee of my pity party, made me lose sight of how my addiction hurt others. The kicker was that my sons had no idea what was going on. At times, they likely felt it was them, not me. Then their mother would come home and be the comfort they needed and that playful soul they craved.

Those bad days would eventually end at bedtime. The next day would return to normalcy, as much as I could expect from myself. Teaching my boys French was part of making them ideal for dual citizenship and future visits to France. More than that, it helped them get to start to talk with their mémé. "Je t'aime, mémé." I love you, Grandma. And my mother really is steadfast in speaking French as much as possible everywhere but definitely at her home. Life extended beyond French lessons though. How does an alcoholic father appease his sons and give them signs to show he cares? For me, it was giving them everything they needed and a whole lot of stuff they didn't. They were so spoiled and this didn't bother me then because it helped to get me by, maybe earn a free pass. Today, it's regretful. Yes, my own life of plentitude and privilege was also going to be theirs. The problem was I spoiled them to compensate for my shortcomings, and this was new and unfamiliar territory. Giving them things to make up for what I lacked was easier than other choices. When I was unable to be what they truly needed, especially with quality time, I hoped a gift would appease them and make me feel better for a second.

After my wife returned home from a long and busy day, I'd be cooking dinner and enjoying a glass of wine, acting as if it were the first one of the day. However, it came after a long day at home and I was ready to decompress. I thought I was "sneaking one by" on my family, or at least that's the lie I chose to believe. It was never about them but they were impacted regardless of if I had a good day or a good night. Let me explain: The better the day was, the more I needed alcohol that night; the worse the day was with drinking, the less inclined I was to tie one on that night.

My behaviors were indicators to me about how I could pull it together for just so long before failing, and I know others saw these shortcomings without necessarily knowing how to categorize them. It would have been hard because I was becoming more secluded, wanting to isolate myself from others' judgment or critique. Talk about a situation to make you paranoid; add that I didn't work an outside job, and I was digging a hole deeper than the Grand Canyon for my mental well-being, plus physical health. Addiction takes its toll on the body and mind.

With my wife, her patience finally wore out and she started to gain control of what she could do, starting with admitting what a farce our marriage had become. Let's be blunt; it sucked when she canceled all my golf memberships. Expensive wastes of time that created opportunities to get drunk; at least that's what they were thought of as to her. To me, these memberships were my only social outlets, and cutting them off meant I was cutting off any adult social contact I had. And guys don't do an occasional spa day for their reprieve, at least none that I know. Even a great spa day doesn't come to a couple of thousand bucks a month as my golf memberships did. We also shared a single checking account and I had one credit card to use, so everything was tracked. That was bad news when it came to my purchasing habits for alcohol. There was no way I could hide things from a wife who had the major work asset of being an accountant. Nothing got by her but damn, I sure tried.

My wife's tightening grip on money was problematic to me, not an act of fiscal responsibility on her part. I'm not sure if that stressed me out more, necessarily. Her mathematical skills did make me more desperate to concoct new conniving ways to purchase my fix. She was casting out a reel and trying to bring me in, not out of hatred but in hopes I'd get an idea of the damage I was doing to my family. With my desperation came a newfound ability to be resourceful. I put out my creative best efforts all the time, especially when my own heavily monitored finances fell short. It's sad and pathetic to admit I stole from my sons' piggybanks for booze money at times, even if it was just enough for an airplane bottle shooter to get me by for an hour. Sneaking into their rooms, thankful for a plug on the bank instead of having to break the bank. I'd count out their small bills and quarters, whatever it took to get the money I needed. Next always came the promise to return those funds and never touch the bank again. Talk about setting yourself up for a failed promise, with two people you loved infinitely more than yourself. Swindling my sons, taking advantage of their youth to rob their piggybanks, was a foul thing to do.

Despite my digressing in life, my sons grew into fine young boys, ready to begin school. I imagine this made my wife relax a bit because of her uncertainties about me. It was a relief to me as well because it took a bit of pressure off my secrecy. Thoughts of going back to work teased my mind now and again and I did make some investments. Mostly, I remained unconfident that I could make it functional through a workday. This thought persisted, which made it as good as real for me, so I continued to be the stay-at-home Papa for my sons. I'd drop them off at school in the morning without issues, and then I could just tend to my wellness and obligations all day long before picking them up.

Everything should have become easier and more manageable, but I managed to make a hot mess out of the process. Increasingly, I was late in picking them up. No more front of the pickup loop with them first in line; it was the back of the line, often the very last car. Nothing had to be the way it was, but it could only change if I did. And while being first in line may not sound like a big deal, it's a perfect way to describe how I went from kind of great at it to mostly late. It didn't have to be that way and shouldn't have been. Feeling that way was numbing, yet substantially less traumatic to me than those times when my sons were in the car with somebody legally intoxicated. I have no idea how many times it happened, and I know even just those few blocks were bad risks to take. I'd white knuckle that steering wheel and pray to get home safe. I'd never do it again if He just got me home safe that one time. And I meant it until it happened again.

Then we'd arrive home and pull into the garage, and my mind temporarily flitted to the next day and what I had to do. I'd look at the hidden bag of emptied booze bottles I had to dispose of at a public garbage. Then I'd think about when I could walk out to meet the alcohol delivery service down the road the next day because it was easiest to keep it a secret if no one saw the delivery car. All of these pathetic thoughts in mere seconds! Then we would go inside, and I'd try to be a present Papa, only to fail at this more times than succeed, in my mind at least.

There were so many times when a confession of my problem was on the tip of my tongue but sucked back in because I chickened out. The words never came out and I was a coward about it because there was no easy or effective way to express such a problem to young boys in a way they could understand. My sons were my driving force in life, the only ones who I felt were worth fighting for during my rare moments of clarity.

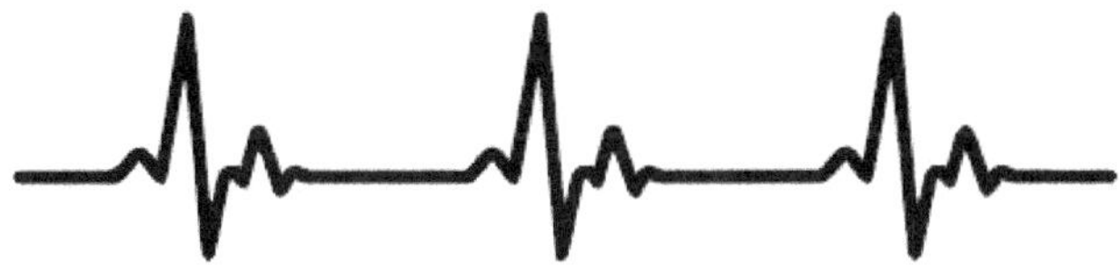

Jan D. Hull was a former Arizona governor who ran a lot of child initiatives she worked to achieve during her tenure. I feel the weight and impact of her words about the most overwhelming important key to a child's success is the positive involvement of parents. Unless you've lived it, it is impossible to understand the anguish that an addict like me has over not being the best for my sons, and I am grateful they have a mother who has always been there for them, addiction-free and determined to succeed.

Being obsessed with keeping the severity of my addiction a secret was one of the strangest obsessions I have ever had. I never realized all the moral implications that accompanied secrets, impacting everything from relationships to work to just adhering to a standard of living that you could feel positively grounded in.

Toxic secrets head to deceit and dishonesty for people, mounting tensions and playing up deceptions. It's a harshly learned lesson that will take a lot of attention when it comes to my sons. I want them to not fear being honest instead of keeping shameful secrets about the areas in which they are vulnerable. Like a lot of parents say: "I want them to be better than me." Just one thought about my boys and I know they already are. If my journey can help them see living proof of how an addiction can be so destructive, I'll consider myself a most fortunate man. If you have secrets, you probably feel how they are eating at you little bits at a time. I feel we all have secrets, and some are okay to keep, but the ones that aren't can be hard to identify, making it so we don't understand what they are doing to us and in our lives.

A hint I've discovered that may help a person in need to better understand how they may be impacted by secrecy is to evaluate how much that secret loops through their mind; if it consumes a person a great deal of the time it is likely something meant to be revealed so you can work through it. I thought about my addiction and its impact on my sons and marriage a lot, but I lacked the courage to confess my truth—I was hurting and struggling.

There is also a practical side to secret keeping, which is called a "utilitarian perspective." I was more about this than I would have realized because I wanted to maximize my happiness and minimize my suffering and others' too. This was my way of justifying secrets, hoping on a wing and a prayer they would result in the greater good. What you know doesn't hurt you, right? It would be great if this were so but it's untrue.

It seems to me that what people don't know is often kept in the dark for nefarious reasons, such as what alcoholism lays the groundwork for. When it comes to socializing, there is no problem showing you drink, but hiding an addiction is a major source of concern. Where other people could have a drink or two, then stop before things got out of control, that first drink or two for me was my warmup. I was seldom alone, but as new buddies showed up at a bar or the golf club, I always treated my drinks as that warm-up one or two. To frame the foolishness of this, I never considered that the bartender definitely knew. Obviously, they did, and it was just through a fluke that my secret wasn't broadcast out in some capacity, especially the clubs that let you put your drinks on a tab that was paid monthly. It would have disrupted me but embarrassment would have just sent me to the next bar because drinking was the primary objective.

When I evaluate the wild cycle of my justifications, this interplay between secrecy and alcoholism reverts back to my lack of authenticity and willingness to engage in self-deception. Only by overcoming my desire to guard my addiction's severity was I able to start working on recovery in a practical sense.

When in recovery if you aren't real, the recovery isn't lasting. The stigma and shame stick to you like the smell of a dead seal you pass by on the beach (which I experienced when writing this). Denial and avoidance became so commonplace you callously toss out any lie to deny or excuse to avoid what's real—you're an addict.

Nothing is left unimpacted by the secrets that addiction holds within its grasp. Families are destroyed. Relationships are ruined. You are left feeling incomplete and devalued. There's more than enough hurt to go around for everyone because the victims of alcoholism are those who deal with it.

Alcoholics are not victims of this disease but products of it. In the end, something has got to give or you will find a barrier bigger than the coral reef between you and recovery. The psychological stress will weigh you down until you feel so small and are stuck inside one of those bottles of booze; it's prisoner until you make a breakthrough. It's surreal to think all this starts with clinging to a secret that you may have a problem with alcohol. Think about it; what secrets do you keep? Do they have consequences made worse by your insecurities?

# 10 || Replaced and Cast Out

*Trust can be broken in a few seconds, but it takes years to heal.*
**—Rei Anthony Albon**

I suspected it but certainly didn't plan on hearing it that day. "Derrick, there's clearly something going on, and you're not making any sort of progress." The meaning was clear; my drinking was worsening, and I was no longer someone to be trusted with making sure my sons' needs were being met. The realization of being fired from being a papa hit me hard. There was a certain amount of denial, but it was quickly cut down the day the au pair arrived. I'd been replaced. The more tragic part was that I didn't blame my wife for doing what she could to protect our sons. They were technically fine, and you can't shelter kids, but you don't have to roll the dice with their wellbeing. My wife was sick of me and sick of standing by, helpless to my struggles; for at least one part of life, an au pair was the solution.

Admitting this failure rattled my core and brought out feelings of shame and, honestly, relief too. A sluggish, often drunk guy couldn't keep up with a prepared, young, energized Brazilian au pair. My journey of self-loathing had grown more intense throughout the years, and it went into hyperdrive with news of her arrival. I was a loser in a toxic relationship, holding a less-than-stellar status as a parent. I felt like nothing. There wasn't a thing I contributed to my marriage, my sons, or our finances. Just by showing up, the au pair was already doing more. I knew it wasn't her fault, and thankfully, being a jerk wasn't among my problems. Fleeing them was more my style, so I retreated to my office on the other side of the house. "I'm looking for work," I claimed. "I'm doing some work," I lied. All these excuses for why I chose to be isolated in my office flowed easily, just as easily as the vodka did. What had I done? What was I doing? I'd ruined everything.

My wife had reasonable expectations of me, and I'd never lived up to them. At least I waited until she left for work to run to my drink, usually to satisfy a craving and stop my dry heaving and shakes. Once vodka started to work its magic, I finally felt my first sense of normalcy for the day.

I looked for jobs to appease my wife, sabotaging myself from receiving any opportunities, always justifying why a possible job wasn't a good fit. The thought of going to work made me want to drink even more.

There was great responsibility in being a father that I constantly managed to fall short of. It was a pathetic day when I faced knowing my sons had never known me sober, at least not that they could remember.

The saddest part of my life was when my wife low-barred her expectations of me. With nobody expecting anything from me, I felt all my purpose had been depleted. I had sunk deeper into my despair. I failed at every bar set for me. No job. No joy. No sense of self.

With the au pair's diligence and presence, I no longer had to try anything. I thought, just get out of the way, Derrick. You're useless. This new depth freaked the shit out of me too often, and it scared me to know I wasn't even at rock bottom. How much worse could it get? I quickly found out. When you stop caring, you get clumsy. I left my hidden bottles in some bizarre places and revealed their presence like a reporter exposing corruption. The cereal cabinet became a holding cell for my booze because I was often so drunk I'd just toss it there or forget to put it away. I'd walk past the cabinet, set a bottle down on a counter, and forget where it was until I heard, "Derrick, what's this?" I always knew what the sound of that voice meant—sadness, disappointment, frustration, and probably exasperation too.

In contrast to the au pair, I had nothing going for me to bring value to my family. She was structured and organized; those two concepts intimidated me because they were impossible to adhere to. The au pair also kept a good schedule that was beneficial to my sons; my schedule was focused on sneaking away to get alcohol. Maybe I'd go to my car and get a bottle from my trunk stash. Once in a while, I'd go out to the bush in the yard and grab the one I hid there. Plenty of times, I forgot where I hid my fix altogether, and I'd have to figure out how I was going to satisfy the urge.

Then came the next wave of bad news for me. It began with my wife needing a medical procedure to take preemptive measures to help her prevent the breast cancer her mother endured. In order to recover and be comfortable, I agreed to take the couch so my snores wouldn't disturb her. This was the start of the end—I never returned to the marital bed after that day. A sleep study later revealed the cause of my snoring: I received the rare diagnosis of sleep apnea despite being relatively young and not overweight. Oops, I had forgotten to mention to the doctor that I had been drinking a lot the whole week leading up to the test. You know the question: How many drinks do you have in a week? My conditioned response was three or four, a lie I easily spewed out, avoiding the reality that it was more than what I could count. It likely played a role in a false diagnosis, but that was an unimportant detail in my eyes.

I brought home my CPAP machine and put it on at night, only to rip it off in my sleep. It was so fucking uncomfortable. And when I tried to return to the marital bed, my wife had a new reason for me not to be back there: The machine was loud and disturbed her sleep. I swear it was quiet, but she said it wasn't.

Being cast out of the bedroom was the final straw in the demise of our relationship, severing any last bit of love and passion for me. All intimacy and connection were gone, and instead of my wife on the pillow next to me, my bottle of vodka was tucked under my pillow.

My isolation overwhelmed me. I tried to hide my makeshift bed, which was either on the couch or the floor, from my sons and the au pair. But who was I really fooling? And did it even matter? This was my pride and determination not to admit how upside down my life was and how out of control I was with my actions. Eventually, something was going to give way, and when that breaking point arrived, watch out. I had no idea what would happen or how I would respond, but its impending presence felt like a vulture circling overhead, waiting for its injured prey to die.

My days on the couch turned into weeks, months, and years. Despite being broken, I remained a physical guy with needs for intimacy that were not being met and a wife I wanted to love but couldn't. In my stupor, it would have been easy to blame my wife, but I had no one to blame besides myself. That was one of the few lies I couldn't sell myself on because its evidence was laid out before me each night as I prepared my makeshift bed. No one trusted me anymore in my house. When my son asked me to quit drinking for him, I said, "Yes." There was no way I was going to tell him I couldn't do it, so I lied to him, knowing it was a lie but selling a good truth, and the next day, I was drunk.

Not being trusted is one issue that leads to exacerbated symptoms for addicts and others who have found themselves in the untrustworthy camp. My sensitive nature was working against me during this time because I obviously didn't care about myself but wanted others to care about me. Yet, I experienced rejection, loneliness, and isolation from those I loved—and it was my fault. Who had abandoned who? These intense feelings were a result of all the damage I'd done, and they led to me being sadder than I'd ever been up to that date and increasingly more resentful of myself. Yelling at others wasn't my problem; beating myself up with a fine stream of verbal abuse was. I was a head case from my self-abuse, and the only way to shut me up for any period of time happened by the way of inebriation.

With trust dissipating out the window like a stream of vapor and no one on my side, I retreated into a shell. If conflict were possible in any situation, I simply left before it could begin. These lows forced me to contemplate questions I was desperate to avoid. Should I end my life? Would that choice be taken out of my hands from my addiction? Could I ever restore myself to someone who had fewer struggles? Every answer was a negative—a reaffirming, "I doubt it, Derrick." If thinking personally degrading and miserable crap was a job, I was a star performer at it. I'd celebrate my performances with a lot of 100-proof Smirnoff, a personal favorite. Each day and night would end with the same repeated beratements. Was this what my life was meant to be? Unloved. Rejected. Failure-filled. Depressed. Not trusted. Liar.

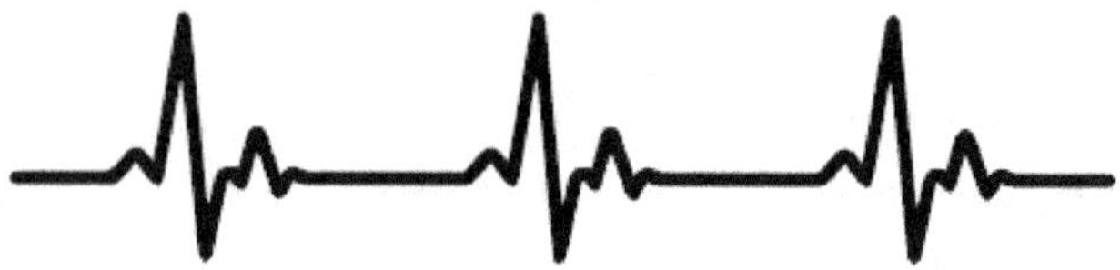

Think about it…if it only takes a few seconds to break trust but years to heal it, how much time do you have to make things right? None of us know how much time we will be given to right our wrongs or regain the trust we've lost. It may never happen, which makes Rei Anthony Albon's quote a bit more optimistic than what I felt when I first began my recovery process.

When an alcoholic is forced to acknowledge uncomfortable truths, such as they are no longer needed or wanted by their loved ones, it is distressing, usually the result of those hurt parties losing trust in you.

For those who have felt this way due to their own actions, whether related to addiction or something else, when the realization comes home to roost, it can lead to deep shame and embarrassment. It leaves you lost and forlorn. Really, all you can do is approach each day with good intentions of making things right for you so you can attempt to make amends with those you may have hurt. The effects of isolation bring people to a depth of despair, unlike anything I've ever witnessed before. At times, I chose to remain alone, wallowing in shame and afraid to look at others, just in case I'd see something to affirm my pathetic nature. One look into my sons' eyes, and I would think they were better off without me. At other times, they made sure I wasn't a part of what they were doing, no longer able to handle my broken promises and shortcomings. Not to beat a dead horse, but all of this comes back to authenticity's role in a lasting recovery. You are who you are, so acknowledging your realities—even those harsh ones—is important to you and your journey of self-love and acceptance. Doing this can hurt so intensely that you feel like you're killing yourself from facing the pain you're living. At times, the thought of self-actualization in your situation feels impossible to work on. In essence, you are rejecting yourself, and if you do that, who can accept you as you are? I have found this answer to be no one.

Rejection is a bitter medicine of the mind that leads you down the path of every moral and ethical decision you ever made, whether favorable or floundering. Find solace in the fact that no one in this world has made all favorable decisions, just as no one has made all unfavorable ones. Alexander Pope, a poet of enlightenment, said, "To err is human," and then ended the quote with, "To forgive is divine." And forgiving yourself is divine, but it requires the hard work of self-reflection to see things clearly from what they are, even if you do so like an outsider looking in, so you don't have to feel the pain at first. In time, you will need to feel the pain in order to understand it and heal from it. Then there are others, and with them, forgiveness isn't guaranteed. We can just do our best, and only we can determine if we did. My identity was cemented in being a father and a husband. These were titles I claimed to be important despite my failings. I wish I would have cared more about my actions than the titles. I'd never met anyone who I believe failed at these tasks more epically than I did. No matter what excuses I made about my wife being toxic to me, I still saw myself in the mirror daily. Therefore, I couldn't avoid looking at myself altogether and realizing I was a subpar husband and father. Okay with saying I loved others but was horrible at demonstrating what love should look like, especially to my sons, who needed a mentor, disciplinarian, and integrity-filled honest man as a father. I brought none of these qualities at my worst times. We all have to call our actions out for what they are, even when we are non-present emotionally; we must show we are engaged in our present moments with others.

German philosopher Friedrich Nietzsche discussed a concept known as "Amor Fati" in his work. The concept behind this is that we all love our fate, no matter how harsh it may seem, and it can still provide us with a coping mechanism in times of need. It's hard to imagine an alcoholic loving their condition, isn't it? I have to admit, I must have loved it on some level because it brought me comfort, calmness, stability (I always knew what to expect), and a quieted mind.

Embracing rejection in order to accept my story was easier when alcohol proved to be a powerful motivator for me. Only when I learned to replace alcohol with other means of showing that I loved my new fate was I able to become repulsed by it. That's what I remember during those moments when the temptation flickers in my mind, and digression feels more inevitable than progression in my recovery. If you're in early recovery, you may recognize when you are leaning toward returning to the ways of old on any given day. This feeling may never subside, and being okay with that is what I've found to be most effective. Those who allow themselves to digress are already breaking ties with their recovery. No alcohol is required! This leaves us with a decision to either accept our digression or fight like hell against it to progress in our new lane of self-love, mercy, and self-compassion. Recovery meetings are there to support us in these types of challenging moments, and for that I am grateful.

# 11 || Pulling Out the Fuckit Card

*I don't care who you are, life has challenges.*
**—Tom Cruise**

Even an alcoholic reaches their limit, not with their ability to consume drink but with their desire to even pretend to care any longer. This "me against the world" mindset exposes someone with addictive behaviors to the liberating and necessary concept called "fuckitmoments." These are the moments when you stop caring because it's easier than dealing with disappointing yourself and others. If my fuckitswere a dance card, it would be all filled, mostly with moments I barely remember and many shameful regrets.

One defining moment is considered the official kickoff of my "fuckit phase." No longer caring, unsure of what would happen next, one decision was made for me. I was in the hospital for a detox when my wife had divorce papers served on me. In the hospital! It felt fucking cold to me, I admit. Yet, when would have been the right time for her? I was always drunk...maybe at least in the hospital, there would be someone to watch over me. I wasn't suicidal, but I was certainly prone to near death experiences by alcohol. And in my heart, I had to admit that I'd already said fuckit about my relationship with her ever being reconciled.

After I got out of the hospital, the next eighteen months were tough on me; I had no wife, lost custody of my sons, and felt like I had no purpose. These feelings of worthlessness were dealt with by my consumption, and I'd never thought it could be worse, but it sure as hell became worse. Imagine passing out mid-fairway on a golf course. How that even happened will be a mystery to me, a moment that cannot be answered. I was golfing alone for one, obviously in a stupor. Did I have control over deciding to lie down, as if it seemed like a good nap spot? Oh, this lush green grass is calling me to lie down on it and absorb its energy. And what must that have looked like when I just flopped down to the ground. It makes me blush, even mentioning it to this day. It also got me banned from that golf course for quite a while; they didn't need people doing such a thing, tarnishing their reputation and holding up the game for others. It was a classic case of where I said "fuckit" to the world, even to golf, which I immensely enjoy.

What really is crazy about getting to this point is your mindset. On one hand, it's an unknowing plea for help. Someone help me see the light! On the other hand, it is a sign of fear, which plays perfectly into the acronym for FEAR, known by people when they're feeling low—Fuck Everything And Run. The FEAR was strong in me, and for some time, it was my modus operandi for life, the way I handled everything. Avoid people. Avoid conflict and run like hell. To put it into perspective, you could be a runner in a race, blitzed off your gourd, or you would set record numbers if someone were chasing you, demanding accountability or demanded an answer. That's what I felt like; my mindset had fully accepted a desire not to fight anything. If you don't fight, you can't lose, right? I bolted from life because it sucked so badly, finding solace in a blur of activities, most of which I do not remember. But I was a winner because I drank my problems away. Seriously, I believed that because it got me by for the moment. At times, when I craved power and felt like I had none, the answer was to go out into an isolated area and shoot my guns. They made me think I was in control and helped me to destroy a target rather than just my psyche. When I started just disappearing for days at a time, sometimes sleeping in my car in strange places, I'd have my gun for protection. Now, that was a big disillusion! I'm ever grateful nothing stupid happened. I can't claim the exact odds, but imagine they're quite favorable that if someone broke into my car, I wouldn't have woken up to be any the wiser. Once I was out for the count, I was out with my fuckit face on and in a deep sleep.

Because everything around me went to shit, I surrendered to the overwhelming weight of the world and took alcohol with me for the ride. I knew addiction better than myself or anyone else, and there was no way out for me in sight. Shit had become meaningless. I basically abandoned any hope for change or redemption. Why would someone bother changing when everything seemed destined to fail, or an action was rendered insignificant? It was a bleak existence I was living, and alcohol was my flame: I felt unlovable except by her. Her love was always unconditional.

Even my parents, whom I love dearly, were victims of my abuse. Isolating them was a positive thing for me because I wanted to protect them from seeing who I'd become, especially at my lowest points. However, during this time, my "fuck itfuckit" attitude and tendency to go dark scared them deeply. They had no idea about the extent of what was wrong, and no help they might offer would work. I was an insignificant smudge that I wanted the family to ignore for their sake. This carried over to my sons. They would be better off without a flawed person around. I just knew it, and there was no way to tell me differently—not that my wife would have. It felt like an unachievable dream, like winning the lottery, to be deeply present for them. I was beyond gone, a cursed soul wandering aimlessly in my northern California world. And that hurt so damn bad, which led to me giving this situation a fuckit salute for my sons' sake. Having them see me in the gutter could not happen because it could tarnish their innocence.

With my sons and my parents, I now know that what I was doing at that time wasn't the great act of self-sacrifice that I thought it was. My life worked only by being in self-preservation mode. I had no answers, but I sure didn't want anyone else to realize this. The easy route was the only one worth considering—I knew this but would never admit it. Fleeing the scene was my favorite move. I could go dark and off grid just like a spy, but nothing was intriguing or cool about it. I was sick and hurting. On one occasion, it took the minds of four siblings to triangulate my location. I was the missing person they were in a crunch with time to find, and they only hoped I'd still be breathing. They did find me passed out in the back seat of my car near my home. I'd returned from a fishing trip and had a flat tire, which I could not change until morning.

The fuckit card is beneficial at times but not in times of desperation. I used it as a pass to become lawless and rogue. Everything was up for debate and challenge. What was the point of following rules? They were like chains that kept me in a reality I didn't want to be a part of. All the norms of what I viewed as a shit world didn't work for me because they confined me to what I hated. My thoughts were that going rogue and enjoying freedom were the only way to even have a chance at surviving this trainwreck, even if they made me a builder of my mental prison instead of the liberator of my addiction. So, yes, to everything I faced or was fearful to address, I embraced the "fuckit policy" just to survive in those toughest years before my last rehab.

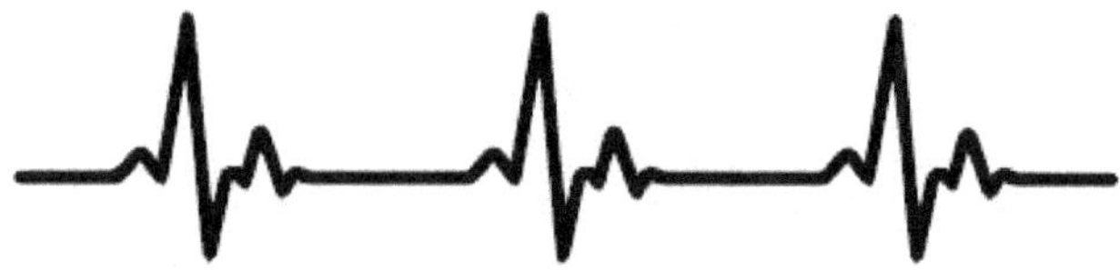

I've never thought of Tom Cruise as a great philosopher, just a Hollywood actor. When I saw his quote sharing that everyone has challenges, it actually provided me with a sense of relief. For so long, I felt like I was the only one constantly challenged, day in and day out, for what I did or didn't do, how I responded, or avoided responding altogether. I'd stacked the deck against me, and it was kicking my ass.

My solution was to sign up for the fuckit path forward and stop trying to please myself or others, as it was doomed to failure.

This concept is not new to me, but it is one that has existed in our world for nearly all of time. It's called nihilism, and it is the philosophical belief that life lacks inherent meaning, value, and purpose. There is a serious lack of inspiration in this definition for somebody with an addiction they're battling. Why wouldn't you want to choose the addiction over the battle? It's a whole lot easier to stick with addiction when you're down and out, void of a purpose to become better. Nihilism asserts that traditional values and beliefs are unfounded and that there is no objective basis for truth and morality. For me, those first tries at rehab that I took were viewed as money grabs for them, not concern for me. That's what I sold myself on, and if you believe it, it feels true whether it is or not.

Then there's the depression factor, which exists in everyone with alcoholism, at least, I feel it does. You don't throw life away when you sense your purpose and role within it. Instead, you enter a place where you feel life is devoid of purpose, any effort to act contrary to this is a waste of time. I get it today, it's a defense mechanism, a way to attempt to regain control by choosing not to engage in a fight perceived as inherently worthless. When we feel worthless, where do we go from there? How do we start another day on a better foot? When those answers do not come, you will likely grow impatient and stop asking or trying. Instead, you feast on your false sense of worthlessness.

Looking back, I am thankful I was given the gift of being competitive. It got me through quite well for a long time, and when it turned on me, it still worked. I entered a one-man competitive race driven by the concept of not losing. What better way to not lose than to disengage.

This choice allowed me the freedom to not repeat my mistakes because I wasn't going to be anywhere near where they were. Take that! Sadly, many people took on the worry and fear that came with me, fleeting in and out of their lives. For a long time, I was still a husband (on paper anyway), I was a papa too (by name, anyway). I took a step away, turned around, and kept on walking. It's quite ironic I felt abandoned when I knew I was the one who abandoned my sons, and of course, they didn't understand. How could they? Damn, that must have hurt, and it is a part of my journey that is not reconciled yet. I have forgiven myself but the choice isn't mine to make if they choose to let me back into their lives. Well, this destructive disease was of my own doing. In that, I succeeded; it just was not what I wanted. The thing with nihilistic tendencies is they make you feel autonomous about your self-destruction.

You're living out your choice, including succumbing to addiction. I view this as one of the harshest forms of personal agency an individual needs to reconcile with. Have you ever thought a decision to give up on something was actually an exercise in freedom? The choices we make are ours to own, even when they are not the choices our better selves desire. Referring back to my golf club fairway pass out. I made the choice to get that bad, and if I had died from drinking too much, that would have been due to my choice as well. It's no fun to write or admit these things, but they are true.

What can I say about the fickle beast known as nihilism. This destructive stance can start you down a euphoric path of liberation; it always ends at the doorstep of distress. Nihilistic behaviors make nothing better, and for me, they left me feeling like life was pointless, and I was helpless. Both of these are powerful barriers that stop people from acknowledging that they need the help of others.

This sad part of my life helped me meet my lowest points with a keen sense of avoidance. I just wasn't ready to take responsibility, accept what I could not change, and seek out those tools that would help me begin the process. When we feel this way, giving others the importance they may deserve is impossible because we have our heads shoved up the back end of denial. This is why remembering we have value is so important to changing a mindset that tries to tell us otherwise.

# 12 || Casting Shadows

*Nature does not hurry, yet everything is accomplished.*
**—Lao Tzu**

Clear water, beautiful mountains all around, seclusion, and a fly rod in hand is one of the most appealing settings my mind could paint. Whenever I traveled toward the Trinity Alps, I saw this transition from my dream state to reality as I gained distance from the city and access to this pristine area of the world. I'd gone there as a child with my family, also with friends at times, and now I was going there as a divorced man, alone, wanting to escape the harshness of my bitter life. If there was a place that could do it, it was the picturesque beauty of this magical spot combined with the challenge of fly fishing. This is a place that offers beauty, spiritual renewal, and the rigorous discipline it takes to fly fish the waters of the Trinity River. From watching the arc of my cast to thinking about life as my line was in a dead drift, it grounds me like few other things have done. Every challenge I've faced has gained a bit more clarity after a fly fishing excursion, making it so personally powerful despite my smallness in these natural environments.

Three weeks in nature with friends was the initial plan. It ended up being altered to just me. While their plans had changed, my need had not. My camping spot was on some land on the the Trinity River, which a friend owned. A small outhouse with power and a campfire outside—the opposite of a high-end resort yet perfect in its simplicity and setting. My family was concerned about me being alone in this isolated environment. "I'll be okay," I told them. It was with good reason they didn't blindly accept my word for this. They were afraid, unsure of what the hell was going to happen. They had every right to feel this way. I promised to check in when I could, reminding them of the spotty cell phone service. It might be challenging to reach anyone or even text. Still, I felt completely confident I would be okay out there.

For this trip, I left home eager to get past the high-traffic areas and onto the more tranquil, inviting winding roads. A road leading away from civilization was both intriguing to contemplate and exciting to travel. My gear bag carried my fishing necessities and my emotional support alcohol. The only setback for me would be if I hadn't packed enough booze to last for three weeks. The possibility had already been planned for; a small town wasn't too far away.

Pulling onto the secluded dirt road that led toward my riverfront camp excited me. It was the start of the trip, and since it was just me, unpacking was quite easy. I built a campfire and found that its warmth in the fading sunlight was my best companion, certain to keep my drinking just between us. There were days when the water never saw me or my rod because I chose to drink and contemplate life by the fire. Other times, I read from books I hoped would offer me the answers I'd been eluding so long. Mostly, I was lost in all my mistakes. Some I blamed others for. Mostly, I blamed myself.

On the day I decided to take a trek across the river to fish, I felt good; not sober, but good. I drove the car over to a favorite stretch of river, ready to embrace it head on. My goal was to hook into the anadromous steelhead—my favorite fish to go to battle with. My mind was relaxed, and I wondered what it felt like to have a relaxed mind more often than not. As I cast out time and again, I had a long discussion with myself about how each cast was kind of like an act of faith. A hope that, despite the odds, it might be the day where everything aligns. This was a positive thought, and I held on to it tightly all day because it made me feel good, a previously foreign emotion to my tumultuous life.

Finally, with no fish caught but still feeling satisfied, the pouring rain cautioned me it was time to head back to camp. My trek back across the river commenced, and I didn't have a care other than focusing on each step I took; there was no reason for me to think I wasn't equipped to make it. I had no choice but to make it, so.

I began crossing the river, feeling confident because it wasn't something new to me. I'd done this a great number of times in my life. I knew the river deserved respect, so it would be kind to me. My foot took a step forward, only it didn't stop on a rock. It kept going, and I found myself sunk into a hole. It was hard to process how a familiar act turned to "oh shit" in the blink of an eye. My arms flailed about to grab something (there was nothing), and I was thrown off balance. I flopped to the ground, and my body slammed backward onto the rocks, my back pounding into them. It was a mighty thud followed by instant seething pain.

Moving wasn't possible right away. I was startled and assessed what had happened to me. My foot plunging into the hole was foreign, an invasion. My ability to process details was interfered with as the pain pulsated through my body. I yelled out a few choice words. Everything was blurred, and I lost control of my actions for a period of time. How much time, I do not know.

Then, I was impacted by nature's touch—something out there helped me come back to the present moment. I managed to stand up, get my foot out of the hole, and waded across the remainder of the river, which had turned its angry wrath on me. When my car came into sight, I felt relief. I went back to camp and stayed another night, drinking away the pain, hoping I'd feel better in the morning.

Morning brought me no relief, the pain was worse, and it had become unbearable. Alcohol offered no relief, and my ankle looked so busted, completely bruised, and contorted from the swelling. My back hurt like hell. My entire body writhed in agony, including my head. With no sense of order, I tossed my belongings into the car and began to drive toward the closest regional hospital.

A nurse stared at me, both in disbelief and with compassion. A man who looked as bad as he felt, that's what she saw. A few x-rays and an exam later, I received my diagnosis: I had a broken back with three compression fractures to go with the broken ankle. The pain of these injuries was followed by the embarrassment of having to admit something else impacting me. I was about to go through withdrawals, and I could sense it coursing through my body and exiting my limbs like small shockwaves. I had to get out of there. They described me some Ativan, which I accepted but knew I shouldn't have because I was drunk and certainly not under anyone's care. For those not familiar with Ativan, it is a sedative that works on the central nervous system to alleviate symptoms of anxiety, agitation, and seizures that accompany withdrawal. It helps to stabilize the brain and central nervous system. It is serious shit, and it was left in my hands to manage. Another act of God's grace ensued. I left the regional hospital, telling them I had a ride. Four plus hours later, I was in Monterey, knowing I needed a better hospital despite my impaired and despaired state. This was my second saving of the day. The staff immediately took action by detoxing me under their supervision and getting me the right boot fitting.

I never told my parents the full story of that day. They were relieved I was okay, and I was not about to give them the details so they could have further evidence I was as bad as they likely presumed I was in the throes of my addiction. It really was shocking, and making it out of there, all things considered, is miraculous.

That was my one bad experience in the Trinity Alps. As horrific as it was, it will never supersede the incredible memories and experiences this wonderland has brought to my life, and it still does. Nature keeps you humble just as much as it unleashes its fury. Some of the memories are thought of so warmly because they are fun, such as those times when I'd be fishing with my buddies, floating. The first person to catch a fish was the first one to have a pull from the flask. Of course, I always had my hidden flask with me and never started any part of my day or vacation without a little "eye-opener."

Then, there were the challenges that came with fly fishing. I was delighted with how they made me look at a situation differently from all angles. I typically fish for Steelhead trout—the "fish of a thousand casts." It's elusive and ever-challenging, known for its strength, speed, and acrobatic leaps once hooked. These fish are notoriously difficult to catch, requiring patience, skill, and a deep understanding of their behavior and habitats.

I've spent endless hours using different techniques and presentations to garner a Steelhead's attention. Fishing under an indicator. Swinging flies. The thrill of finally hooking a steelhead after countless attempts makes the pursuit incredibly rewarding. I have always felt honor and exhilaration in the challenge of the fight. If I demonstrated that same tenacity and will to endure the fight with the rest of life, would it have made a difference?

Contrary to the calming effect of fly fishing, it can also be an incredibly aggressive sport. It allows those who love it to test limits in high risk ways. This was a thrill I latched on to. Crossing angry, swelling rivers, not seeing the river bottom, and relying on the hope my wading jacket would keep me floating down the river boots up tested my quick thinking. Always holding my precious fly rod over my head and protecting it along with my flask was a challenge I wouldn't dare fail at.

At other times, it was me against nature on my single-man pontoon. I'd read the water ahead and see danger but kept on moving toward it because of a brazen approach to life fueled by liquid courage. Kind of weird to reflect on this. What was it exactly? Why did I have less fear than I probably should have had in those situations? I knew the threat was fucking real, but I didn't care. Thoughts of mortality didn't exist. Some may feel this was morbid; I find it to be enlightening because it was a reminder of the impermanence of existence for everyone—not just an alcoholic. It somehow made me more alert than at any other time. When I'd go warm up and drink more at day's end, vivid recollections of the experiences were my joyful companion. I didn't forget any of these details, and the shit happening around me felt almost superficial compared to the rage of man against nature. Really, when I am on the water fly fishing, it becomes more than just about me. I've always been grateful for that. Whether I fished gracefully or awkwardly, I was always connected to the world around me. Even if I got skunked, I felt joy. If the river was good to me that day, landing just one fish made every trying moment fade away.

We all need joy in life, a healthy release, and this is what fly fishing offers me. Even on an ideal day with "perfect" conditions, what you seek might not be there, and there isn't a damn thing you can do to control the situation. Controlling nature it's laughable, isn't it?

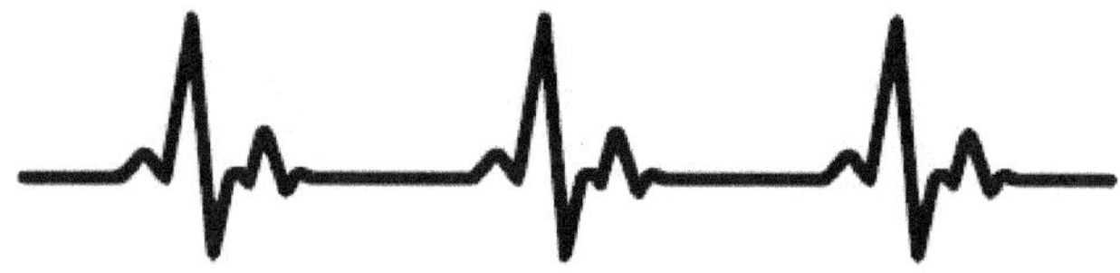

Teachings from Lao Tzu's timeless book, The Art of War, are laden with sound lessons for the strategy of life, not just war. When he wrote about how nature is never in a hurry and still manages to accomplish what it intends to do, I feel he also realized how much this applies to human nature. When fly fishing, no matter how impatient a person might get, they cannot make the fish come to them. This is a challenge you'll lose, which is why patience is so important.

With addiction, there is a strong connection between nature and recovery. A person can find a powerful ally in nature when they are overcoming struggles, learning to accept and embrace the emotional significance of the label "alcoholic," as well as the transformational opportunity that comes from connecting with nature, not just the bottle. I find this necessary release through fly fishing. This works for me, but we all have to find what nature does for us. Hiking, running, biking, et cetera. All I know is that it helps one's life to be more grounded when one finds one's own avenue to this enlightened state of being. Everyone can appreciate nature and heal from its presence. My humble and wholehearted advice to anyone who hasn't experienced a retreat to nature is to give it a try. You'll find a valuable way to restore yourself to a baseline, plus appreciate how nature always acts as it should, free of invasive influences.

At times, I'm overwhelmed with nature and how it impacts my life. I feel that these opportunities to reconnect with simplicity and the authentic self are important, even when I can't fully explain them. The essence of nature facilitates this existential confrontation. It offers a space free from societal distractions and pressures, where one can confront and contemplate the fundamental aspects of their existence. Understanding is gained, and our place in this world becomes clearer. And for me, I realize there are not only fish to be caught on the river but worthy goals to pursue when I return home.

Have you ever tried to change a law of nature? If you did, you know it's impossible—and we should be glad for it. Operating according to its own laws, indifferent to human desires, provides humans with a lesson of how we could approach life. It wasn't always easy for me to understand that I couldn't dictate an outcome just because I wanted it to be a certain way. Knowing I can't do this or even want to do this any longer liberates me. My focus can be on those things which I can do. In a spiritual sense, nature has always been a direct pathway to the divine. When my addiction was at its worst, I'd tend to forget how important this was or just do what I could to avoid any type of deep reflection from haunting me. As I heal and restore personal balance, nature has provided me with endless sources of renewal. Daily walks along the beach make me see my good fortunes and show gratitude for having an opportunity to be sober for the day. Starting my day with a deeper connection to something greater than myself is a great motivator to make the best of it. I can even rebound from tough days much easier now, thanks to the opportunity to use nature's healing powers.

I've also found nature helps me to develop those traits I will require for a sober life in the future. At times, it takes patience, knowing recovery is a step at a time and every day's action matters. That could be overwhelming without patience, which is strengthened by increased resilience. How do I handle a situation today that would have led to me drinking prior? Most always, my answer involves getting out of the confines of my environment—and my head—and taking a deep breath to clear my thoughts and feel the exhilaration of the breath. We can all have a moment where we take our shoes off, dig our toes into the earth, and gain perspective, releasing what constricts us. The courage to do these things makes all the difference to me. I am okay with being mindful and aware of the present moment.

# 13 || Driving on Empty

*I made the wrong decision many times. Sometimes I can accept it... but in the end it depends on yourself and whether you are ready to move on or not.*

**—Dejan Lovren**

It wasn't so long ago, but I still cannot remember if sobriety became a desire, and I snapped my fingers to grant my wish, and then I was ready for the challenge. Or, perhaps, it was a slow brewing decision I finally felt ready to face. All I am certain about was that I was serious about getting sober. Going to rehab would be the start of the end of drinking, the dawn of my new beginning.

There were a few details I needed to take care of before trying. I had gotten so bad that I wasn't cognizant of how often a drunken state had become my norm. The Friday before my Monday admission into rehab, I started taking care of all those details I felt should be addressed before I turned my sights on my new future. With my twenty-eight days in rehab, there would be a period of time when I wasn't allowed to have any outside contact. This would have felt strange since it was initiated by someone else—normally—but it wasn't a concern when it was my decision, which is what going to rehab again was.

Traveling through the winding roads of the Del Monte Forest, I made my way out of Pebble Beach to deliver some medical images from the fishing accident to my spinal doctor. If you thought for a second, I did that sober, you're giving me too much credit for where I was in life at that time. With my fifth nestled next to me, I head out the door. This day was hazy in some ways, but one thing that stood out to me was that it was not a typical sunny day. A storm was brewing, and I was heading into its wrath. It was raining quite hard, and the turbulent air grew windier. Despite the weather's quick turn to darkness, I was going to get those MRI images to the doctor. I'd made it a personal mandate to do so, and no one could have dissuaded me. It was only later on that I learned the entire area I was driving through was at a high risk of an atmospheric river hitting land nearby. It should have been nerve wracking, and a normal guy would have remained at home. By this time, you probably realize my life was anything but the elusive normal.

Nervous and determined, I took the edge off the only way I knew how. To put a weather system like the one I was facing into perspective, imagine a wicked weather condition a thousand miles long like the East Australian Current getting mixed up and ending up in the sky! This type of weather event creates a global distribution of water vapor. If this manages to make landfall, watch out. Not only will you get pouring amounts of rain and snow, but you're also at risk of flooding and whiteout winter storms. All this in California—it's true.

When this weather phenomenon hit that winter, it felt like it sought me out directly and taunted me for what I was doing. Playing with me like I was the mouse and it was the roaring lion. I wasn't about to surrender or retreat, so I just kept moving along down this winding and, isolated road through the forest. No other fool was on the road besides me. But I had it covered and could handle myself. The atmosphere was violent and thrashing; branches whipped around in a wicked dance orchestrated by the wind. Debris was littered all over the road. And then there was me—I felt I could navigate through this. This storm was so loud, and it sounded like the world was caving in on me. What the fuck was I thinking? I sure wasn't thinking a big ass tree would fall down on the road right in front of me until it did. I swerved and ended up crashing my car into a stack of tree clippings the CHP had placed in that precise spot. It was in perfect alignment to wipe out my car as I swerved into it. You would have sworn it was planned that way; well, maybe it was by some force out of my control.

I stumbled out of my car, holding on to it like a sailor might hold the railing of a ship in pouring rain, and knelt down to check out underneath to see what I was dealing with. I figured I'd be able to get the car out, then be on my way—no harm, no foul. Only I couldn't get it to budge. I decided to call AAA. They could send a flatbed out and get it back on the road for me. Before they could even come and try to help me, a police car pulled up behind me. Oh no! I needed help, I know, but the sober feeling I felt my high tolerance had earned me was lost on them. "Have you been drinking?" they shouted through the torrential rain. "No," I said. Keep it short and sweet, I thought.

They took me to the back of the squad car. The only thing nice about that was getting out of the rain. But now I was trapped back there, and they asked me to take a breathalyzer. I refused. And with the field sobriety test, the conditions were such that even a sober person would have faltered outside in those elements. Tactics were switched, and they told me they were taking me to the hospital, that I had injuries which really needed to be checked out. Really, it was a shallow scratch on my face, and it wasn't from the accident but from getting underneath the car to try to get it unstuck. At the hospital, they did a blood draw, and it registered my BAC at .393, nearly five times the legal limit. Most people could enter a coma or die at this level, but for me, I still was kind of alert, which shows how used to alcohol my system was.

My situation didn't look good. I was in a bit of disbelief, my drunken stupor more visible. Before long, I was being taken to jail to be booked and tossed into a cell for the night. I'd sober up, and then they'd release me. By the time they let me go the next day, I was shaking from withdrawals and trying to slither out of the police station undetected—a shamed dog with his tail between his legs. Desperate and defeated on every level, I took a taxi home, with a stop at the liquor store on the way. It was the first day of a new legal battle, one that was foreign to me by good luck alone.

Now, I look at the lousy situation of the DUI as something positive in my life. I had driven drunk so many times and had always gotten away with it, including getting my innocent sons home safely. It became a wake-up call to acknowledge how drunk driving could hurt me and, worse, other people. It shocks me to finally recognize how little regard I could have for life at times when I was drinking.

With court dates to coordinate, my rehab got moved out for a few days. I still have an interlock system on my car to make sure I am sober every time before I drive. Eventually, it will be removed; however, for now, it is a good thing to be reminded of what almost happened due to my irresponsibility. This reminder is more than helpful to me when it comes to sober driving; it also reiterates that alcohol is not something I can enjoy casually. I'll never be able to have a drink or return to being casual with a mixed drink. What drives me today is my pursuit of a more fulfilling and peaceful life in my sober skin. It fits me well, and I'm comfortable in it.

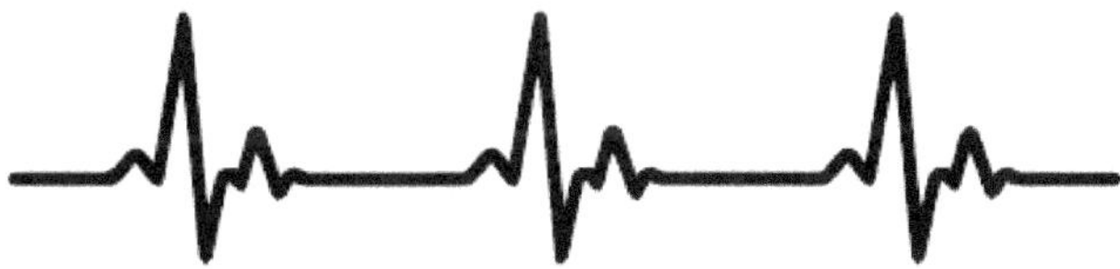

The words of Dejan Lovren really resonate with me on a level associated with my addiction. I've made the wrong decisions more times than I'll ever be able to count. The ones I can't accept or don't forgive myself for are the greatest challenges. Those I accept are ones I can learn lessons from and then move on. I'll never be casual about how I placed my sons and others in danger from my choices. However, I have realized that no matter how hard I "will" my past to change, it cannot.

Reliving the same thoughts repeatedly traps me in the sickness I had, not the solutions I needed. It's up to me to reconcile with it and move onward. What I know is that my daily actions are evidence that I've changed. Who wants to hear me talk about change at this stage? No one. They want my actions to demonstrate I'm a changed man, and that is exciting to me and also damn scary at times, too, I admit. The process is one that latches on to hope but also requires deep introspection in addition to outward demonstrations of achievement. From what I've heard and experienced, having remorse after poor decisions made under the influence is common. Who is glad they placed themselves and/or others at risk? What happens to us when we feel this is okay? I feel it's my moral duty to embrace this. This aligns with philosophical thoughts regarding the fairness and value of the individual. I had to start believing in my own worth again in order to progress with recovery. People do have the ability to reason to preserve their autonomy, even if it is through poor decisions. When I was at my worst, I used alcohol to justify my autonomy, and now, as I find a renewed way to live, I understand my moral decisions and ethical grounding are imperative to this process. It seems this would be a good formula for every person with struggles in their life. It isn't just alcohol that can leave you impaired to better judgment; we all have vices that don't lead to our most rational and moral thinking.

What I often failed to recognize during my drunkest days was that there were so many extremes with me. I didn't always act appropriately, not in a sexual way, mind you, but with my lack of recognition about when drinking was appropriate, such as at a social event. I had no temperance and would gladly sneak away to down a bit just to keep myself even-keeled—even if it was at one of my son's soccer games. I wouldn't have been shocked to enter an AA meeting half lit during this time because my body needed it, and my mind too.

It is only through understanding the graceful compassion that we are all worthy of extending ourselves so that we can face, head on, what we have to be remorseful for. Reliving some of those worst moments was hard, but it was a part of the process of releasing what had me so tangled up for far too many years. Some call this virtuous living; maybe it is. To me, it's not so much about virtue as it is about respect for the human condition—mine and the world around me, too. Empathy has played a huge role in helping me to see my challenges from others' points of view. Today, I understand that bridging the gap between my past behaviors and my future begins with remorse. It is only through the act of being remorseful that we can release that which blocks us from our authentic selves. Are there situations where you find this information could help you overcome a hurdle or an obstacle that has you stuck? Don't be fearful of the pain of the process guiding you true north toward your authentic self; be fearful of avoiding what holds you prisoner in a dark place, a place you long to be free of. Knowing the harm you've caused can become a catalyst for a good outcome, at least enough so you can maximize joy and minimize suffering.

Of course, it's easier to say these things once you've already done things the wrong way. I do understand this. It's not meant as a way to tell you, "Derrick did it. Why can't I?" It's more complex than this, a union of the heart and its intention. Removal of the ego and acceptance that by the grace of God, you are imperfect and always will be, yet you are loved should never be forgotten. Remember, our thoughts are energy that fuels what we give and receive.

Even internalized conflicts are cast out into the universe by the thoughts and energy within you. You don't have to say a word to be out of alignment with the world. And when prayer doesn't help, and mindfulness is lacking, you have to dig deep to reconnect with it. It's actually incredibly exciting to sense how this transformation of awareness takes place, starting with even the most minute change in your mindset. Try going from I can't do this to just "Maybe I can," and you'll already feel better. Don't let personal ignorance of what you're facing—or denying—stop you from seeking the truth that will set you free. It sounds incredibly cliché, yet my life has proven this to be a powerful truth. I never thought this would be the case; and I know I am not alone. We all feel our problems are bigger than anyone else's, and this is a debate that could never be settled, especially without complete honesty.

Regardless, seeking the truth is what will set you free. We are connected to every aspect of the world around us, from nature to an innate desire for freedom. Responsibility doesn't have to overwhelm us, yet it does have to start with us. One decision at a time, we can move from being someone who has lost their identity and lacks purpose to someone who is self-aware and on fire for something that brings meaning to their life. Alcohol never did that for me, not really; helping others understand this is something I hope can help them, just as it helps me solidify my sobriety.

# 14 || Rehab Ping Pong

*Every worthy act is difficult. Ascent is always difficult. Descent is easy and often slippery.*

**—Mahatma Gandhi**

A severe physical reaction. Alcohol intake reduced. Complete chaos erupts from the inside out of your body. These are signs of an alcohol-related seizure. It's one of the most serious and horrific manifestations—make that retaliations—a person's physical being can endure. In fact, it's life threatening. You don't have to hear those words to know the severity of it; you can just feel them. I can be dramatic at times, I admit, but whenever a seizure hit my body, I did believe I was going to die. And in those moments, I knew one thing—I wished to live.

This was what I felt like with my first alcoholic seizure. It came upon me like a flash flood right after my fly fishing accident, and thankfully, it happened when I got to what I call the "real hospital," not the small regional one that first saw me. It happened not long after I was admitted, when I was lying on a bed in triage, and doctors and nurses were swarming around me to start my medical attention. I was barely hooked up to the equipment when the bells and whistles started to go off. The staff freaked out for a moment, then took action to get me through my seismic event. It was a damn long two minutes... I think.

Abruptly stopping my prolonged exposure to alcohol meant my brain got into a state of severe hyperexcitability. This often reveals itself as a seizure. Let me tell you, you don't get much warning when a seizure is set to take over, but when it's done, you're left with confusion, disorientation, and anxiety. It sucks, and it becomes a "get your shit" together warning that lasts for at least a bit of time. Drugs like Ativan are designed to prevent the risk of seizures, and it was good I had that from the previous regional hospital, but it was also not good. I'd lied about my driving, and they hadn't bothered to verify. This is one of the biggest reasons alcoholics are hard to trust; they'll say anything to do what they feel is important to them at the moment, rational or not. Not only was I driving, but I was taking a drug that I shouldn't have had in the car, as it needed to be taken under strict medical supervision. That's how you avoid overdoses and certainly how you can avoid death. The warning labels aren't just for a one in a million chance of death—this medication has more probable odds than one in a million.

Nothing felt good about what I was feeling. Physically, I was beat up. Emotionally, I was a wreck, barely keeping it together. However, I was relieved to make it through that seizure. It felt like I'd been given a second chance. The problem was that second chance could only work without alcohol in my system. So, it didn't last long.

It's hard to say if this type of seizure comes more easily on a repeat performance. I was in for one and had a second seizure not so long after that first one. This time, I was alone in my office space. I cannot recall why I hadn't drunk for a few hours. The details remain hazy to this day. I just know the withdrawals were instantly intense enough that I began to seize and convulse badly. I came to and saw a disaster strewn about. Tables were tossed and turned, and one was even on top of me. I was bruised over my entire body, unaware of how it happened. I pictured how I must have looked, thrashing and flailing, uncontrollable against myself or the assistance of others. My eye was black and swollen. My body ached all over like I'd just taken a punch from Mike Tyson. No one was around me when this happened. This made it the luckiest seizure I had, if there is such a thing. It's an event that is mostly unknown until this telling of it. People in my life had enough to worry about without worrying about this. Their wheels must have been turning in their minds. Did he have another accident? How did he get that black eye? Derrick, WTF!

The last seizure I know I had was one when I was at home, living with my parents again. It is the one that registers the harshest in my mind because it was my mother who found me. I only know what happened here by her account to me after the fact. She was doing something on the main level of the house and heard some unusual noises coming from upstairs. Being a spritely age eighty-seven at the time, she came upstairs and found me. The thoughts she must have imagined she has kept hidden from me. What I knew was that she realized she was unequipped to help me, so she called an ambulance right away. It remains a nightmare to think about her frantic and scared eyes just being able to watch me, not able to get too close because physically I was like the Hulk from the utter violence of the event. Thoughts of this still evoke sadness to this day, not for me but that she had to see her son in such a state.

That day, the hospital detoxed me and then sent me back home. I felt like shit and craved a drink to calm down. It was time to face my life on a want to live versus prefer to die basis. These seizures showed I was nearing the end of the line with my addiction. I either had to sober up for good or risk dying from a seizure or alcohol poisoning. But I wasn't ready to do either—die or quit drinking! However, if the seizures continued to worsen at the pace they were and increased in frequency, it was inevitable. I knew I'd also had seizures that I cannot remember. How else did I wake up in bed with a sprained ankle? Or a bruised and battered face. Nothing was clear or clearly defined in my life any longer, and winging it didn't work.

That's it; I was going to rehab again for my fourth time. It was only when the world was eating away at me, swallowing me up in my own depression, that I'd agreed to try to get better. With my first round at a state rehab facility, I felt forced to go in order to prove I wanted to get sober. I did it to appease my family and loved ones more than out of my commitment to sobriety that I had to make for myself. It would also show I actually was a good guy, not the piece of shit I felt like. With my wife and kids gone and the divorce final, it felt like finding sobriety was a good way to better represent myself as more than a failure. I wanted to be a part of my sons' lives and had shared my desire to be this renewed man for myself and for them. Then, the heartbreaking news that my sons would be moving to the East Coast was delivered, and despite my objections to it, I couldn't fault my ex for it. The series of actions I'd chosen over the years called me out as a liar because I'd done nothing to be the father I claimed to want to be and that my sons needed. On some level, I knew my wife still loved me, but she had to let go for the well-being of her and our sons.

My first attempts at rehab hadn't worked. Every time I left, I'd eventually relapse. I began to doubt I was someone who could actually experience a successful new beginning. Maybe I wasn't even worthy of the chance—who knew. My better chance, the more likely chance, was I'd just drink myself to death. So depressing was that thought that I wallowed in it, drinking more to not worry about what might happen. This type of thinking is common for addicts despite being highly illogical.

Every time I relapsed after trying sobriety, I had some excuse before I'd revert to active addiction. And that's just what those were—excuses. It wasn't the staff or the program, ever, although I tried to say it was at times. The reason was that I was not ready for the next steps because they were hard to take, and my mind fought them. I did not want to quit drinking on some deep level, and so I failed. Admitting I didn't want to stop would have been better because I would have known what I was dealing with. It was slowly becoming a situation where rehab was like a game of ping pong and I'd show commitment for a bit, then my addiction would take back over. I wasn't really interested in committing to help myself yet. Nobody should have had to deal with the disaster I'd become.

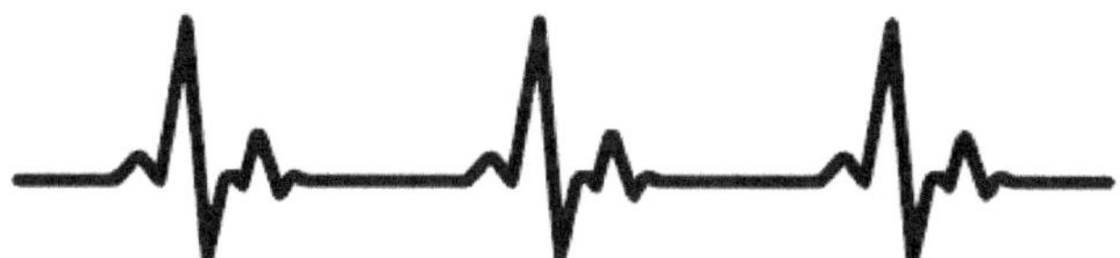

The quote at the beginning of this chapter is from Mahatma Gandhi, and he talks about how our most worthy acts are often the most difficult. Becoming sober was more difficult than I was prepared to face, which made the ascent nearly impossible. I was like a mountain climber who was out of breath after thirty seconds, so I decided to turn back around, just to find an easy descent back to where I'd started and then even lower. Each failed attempt at recovery returns you to a lower point, both mentally and physically. When you reflect on the reasons why you would do something to appease others, such as what the first attempts at recovery are often about, a pause needs to be taken to evaluate why this is.

The journey is not for the faint of heart, as it often takes you down scary rabbit holes that force you to address your authenticity and the nature of human freedom. Make no quibbles about it, addicts are far from free. Personal responsibility and forthrightness are easily messed with when you become reliant on lies to get through situations, using them so much that they become a reality. You could tell yourself the sky is red and genuinely repeat it like it's the truth. Whether others believe you or not doesn't matter; the lie getting you by does.

Life is filled with crossroads that put our desires at odds with others' expectations of us. Yes, to an extent, wanting to demonstrate pleasing behavior to others is necessary. It just doesn't happen when you are attempting this based on lies, deceitfulness, and an unstable emotional level. Alcoholics are unstable; we have a knack for doing things that lead to mental and physical anguish. And for all people, living in a way designed to appease others is no way to live. Plenty of times I've pondered why people keep trying to get me to do things when I repeatedly fail. It is usually because they care and do not know what else they can do besides offer these ideas. Today, I use others' kindness or desire to help me as a reminder to be this way with myself—show some self-compassion. Recently, I came across something interesting. It was brought to my attention through Jean-Paul Sartre's writing. He emphasized the importance of authenticity and personal responsibility because we are condemned to be free. What I reflect on with a statement like this is how our every choice reflects our essence and shapes our existence. Decisions made to satisfy others are often made by those who are living in bad faith, which is a state of being where one denies their own freedom and responsibility by placing it in the hands of others. How often have you done this?

I cannot even count how many times I let others state what they wanted for me because I simply couldn't begin to process it. When it came to recovery, this handing over of my fate, if you will, failed me every time until I took accountability, gained authenticity, and decided to become sober for my sake first and foremost. The rest could only fall into place when I fell into grace with myself.

We all have the ability to flourish in life, which is to say we can all experience true happiness and fulfillment if—and it's a major if—we do this based on our virtues. Taking actions that don't resonate with us in order to appease others is not a key to fulfillment. These aren't good deeds that I refer to. Those big encounters don't resonate with us at the moment, for whatever reason, but will make someone else pleased. This all makes so much more sense in hindsight. Decisions made based solely on pleasing others don't take you down the path to your virtues but guide you away from them.

When our reason, spirit, and appetite are not in harmony, we cannot act justly and live well (as we define it). This is why alcoholism knows no income levels; it is about internal factors more than external circumstances. There have been people in dire financial situations who found joy and were authentic to themselves, just as there are uber wealthy people who are stuck in an internal trap that keeps them at bay from what might fulfill them. We all have a rational part of our soul, which seeks the truth for us and about what is genuinely good for us. This is a fragile place, vulnerable to being overridden by what we cannot control, such as the desire to be accepted or liked. When you've sacrificed your authentic nature to be in this place, has it ever worked in the long term? A time is going to come when you have to return to your flow state—and this can take a long time, making it a daunting nemesis for an alcoholic.

By concerning ourselves with what is within our control, which is our own thoughts and actions—we are doing ourselves (and eventually others) a great service. Some things are going to lie beyond our control, and it is good to acknowledge these things for what they are and not cling to them. No matter what we do, we cannot change the course of something beyond our control. This is why rehab focuses on the individual, not the collective. What thoughts and beliefs do you have that you are rooted in? Know this, and you'll learn a lot about how your mind works and how you can honor your best self, not spit into the wind so it flies back and hits you in the eye.

When standing at the base of a mountain, remember what experience you may have if you reach its summit. You can see the beauty of life from above, appreciating it for the energy and love it radiates on you. If you were to imagine looking down at yourself at the base of that mountain, would you be cheering for yourself to make the ascent to the top?

# 15 || Returning to Ground Zero

*When you control your own thoughts, you control your destiny.*
**—Epictetus**

Adhering to recovery is as much of an emotional victory as digressing from recovery is an epic low point. I entered recovery, telling those who wanted me to go it would be hard (of course), but I would do it. The problem was I never believed it could happen those first times. Each of my shoulders had an angel, one with good intentions and the other one with bad ideations. The good angel declared, "I'm sticking with this," and the bad angel talked to my thoughts. "Bullshit. There's no hope for a different outcome." And until we can find a way to temper the impact of the bad angel, the hold it has on us is massive. This is why I had four failed attempts at rehab. That bad angel and I were simpatico.

Now, I have the benefit of learning some important lessons about how a person starts to revert to drinking despite knowing life is clearly better on the sober side. What I've discovered is there are always clues to be found. They may be so subtle or small, making finding them like searching for a mite in a thick shagged carpet. Others are clues left for you to discover when the time is right. For me, grieving from my divorce and knowing my sons were going to be moving far away made sense. Where I struggled was how to manage those intense emotions without the help of the only counselor I'd known for so long—alcohol. So, I went to pay my bottle a visit, claiming it was just one, and the cycle began all over again. By the next day, my drinking habits always returned to their former glory, and I even upped the ante a bit. Now, I had the guilt of knowing I failed at rehab, too, which drove me to drink more. Nothing numbed me enough, and I was exhausted from everything I had strived to feel. Please, just let me feel something meaningful.

Out of all the hazy life moments I've had, there is something unforgettable about those moments leading up to a relapse. I was always still participating in the plan but started doing things I normally wouldn't do. When I was still without a car, I purchased a bike so I could get around. The people I lived with in the sober living environment (SLE) were ones I didn't really have a good relationship with. It seemed like they didn't want to recover, and it made me uncomfortable to be in my situation, knowing this was my perception of their efforts. I wasn't better or different, but I didn't need to be around those who were casual about not doing well. I still functioned as a guarded, secretive man, which meant isolation was more important than camaraderie. My demons were none of their business. Period.

One time, in my desperation to be alone, I pulled off a feat I would have previously termed impossible. I wasn't supposed to have a car due to driver's license restrictions. I had an old license and somehow was able to rent a car. Giving me access to wheels meant giving me access to alcohol. So I packed my bike up from the SLE and drove over to a divey hotel with rooms to rent—it could have been straight out of a movie. It was that kind of dive joint. But it was safe because I felt there was no way anyone who knew me or might look for me would go to a place like that. (I guess I hadn't learned everything at rehab because that was exactly the type of place they often looked for people.) With my cash stash tucked in my pocket, I checked into a room and then beelined to the nearest bar. I'd decided not to return to the SLE. The experience was okay, but it was over. Different versions of that same scenario hold true for every other "fall of the bandwagon" moment I had, all of which took me from recovering with sober living back to ground zero. Imagine returning to the scene of your crime repeatedly, even when it's bad for you. That was me.

If I were ever to have a chance at lasting recovery, I would need to sever my conviction that I could "have just one" and that it would solve my problems and relax my mind. If only my mind allowed me to think so rationally at the time: admit it, then move on. Thinking about my slip-ups always brought on a variety of emotions. Some days, I justified my efforts. I'd done the work at treatment, and that box was checked. Knowing what I needed to do would make it easier to get back on track—I had the tools now, unlike before. But beyond justifications, sadness was what really dictated my life. I was consumed by these moments that went from sadness to anger to getting drunk and feeling hopeless. My head still hurts when I think of how a wounded person could go through so many emotions in rapid order. If emotions were a firing squad, I was the target.

My logical mind always managed to seep into these relapses and condemned me. You should be at your IOP meeting. Your intentions don't mean a thing. You're pathetic. And I believed the darkness of this logical mind. Its harsh words were damning, but it was true. I should have been at my IOP (intensive outpatient treatment) meeting, and it was pathetic to stop trying like I had. There was no choice left but to stay at the hotel another night and make sure I had enough booze to last me at least a day. It wasn't like I had to be at work; the little bit I had been doing to rehab homes with a business partner had ended. He basically kicked me to the curb—but only after I had already stumbled over it countless times during my active addiction.

What these setbacks did teach me when I finally wanted sobriety was that it was necessary to update the plan. Rehab plans, like most effective self-improvement plans, are not set in stone. They need to be pliable, like Bruce Lee says, "become one with the water." Don't fight against what hasn't worked, but find a way to embrace who you are and heal without losing sight of this.

Choosing to stop dwelling in the past wasn't easy because it was a habit as much as a regret. These habits of nature are hard to break because they feel so authentic even when they're deceiving us to be less than we are meant to be, a spiritually whole person.

Knowing taking a drink wasn't the "next right thing" helped, especially when I was forced to realize that when it had "worked," everything crumbled further. Fighting about the right thing didn't matter; choosing an alcohol-free next thing did. But when I'd think of how inviting just the sound of the twist of that bottle cap to my vodka was, it was hard to remember this; it still is at times. Such is the life of an addict.

Saying fuckit suddenly was less rewarding. It had been so easy before because it gave me liberation from my sources of discontent. Now, it feels lazy, and I no longer want to be lazy about my approach to my life. The fuckits led to throwing up, gagging, gulping, and gasping for air until my body returned to status quo—which was a system running on alcohol. I was so sick of it. Even remembering that vodka wasn't water, despite it tasting like it, was challenging. That was a new thing for me that began after my first relapse. It wasn't until I drank actual water that I realized this. "What is this shit? It's not nearly as good as vodka."

Then there was PAWS, which stands for post-alcohol withdrawal syndrome. PAWS tends to bring out the ugliest side of an alcoholic. Anything can trigger it for a period of time when you're trying to get clean. This includes some of the people you associate with or even love. From cravings to irritability and hostility, these emotions suck, and you cannot control how you lash out from them. Stress, anxiety, and depression shoot through the roof when you're going through PAWS, too. This is particularly challenging when you are already overwhelmed with those emotions. You lose all focus and falter in any attempt at betterment. All you can do is remember that in time, it will pass. You won't be that way forever. Of course, even a single day in this space feels like forever.

But then you get through it, and things clear up. That is where the hope lies.

One of my therapists, who has guided me through much of this information, talks about the 3 Ps of pause, process, and proceed. This is what helps you restore balance and truth to your life. It becomes easier to sense when you lie to support your habit, giving you the space to proceed with a better process. The key to rehab standing a chance at being successful is in the self-care you give yourself during these trying days. In my first recovery I didn't use one of the best tools for me, which was relaxation. It never allowed me to separate myself from the vodka and all my toxic behaviors and just be present in the moment, free from self-judgment and expectations. Learning to relax and be comfortable with myself, in my own skin and not drunk, has been so cathartic for me.

Another important component of rehab is physical exercise, which I benefited from greatly with the personal trainer at my treatment center. Being active has always been something I've done. Focusing on how my body responds to it wasn't what I focused on back then; it was getting past the social anxiety on the golf course or indulging in a fly fishing trip. This is why there is such great power and beauty in the outdoors. It can feed the mind with healing thoughts if the mind allows this to take place. You've got to grant yourself permission!

Trust is another important issue that leads to struggles with someone who is failing at sober living. When trust is broken, it may never be restored. For the parts of this process you can control, just do your best, make amends, and follow the recommendations given. Until I draw my last breath, I will keep working to restore trust with my sons and anyone else I have harmed. When I need something to fight for, thinking of my sons is the most empowering thought I can have. I aspire to learn from those moments where I've fallen in the past and lost their trust yet realized the damage could be turned around. This process is on me, not them.

In all these mishaps and events in my life, I have managed to never fully lose the belief that there is a great spiritual being, God, trying to guide me in the right direction. I'm finally listening! Through deepening this connection, I now realize the greatest help starts with my admission of needing it, and is brought to fruition by a wonderful supporting cast of people who don't want to "fix me" but do want to help me heal. And I see a beacon of hope, which is the day recovery begins again.

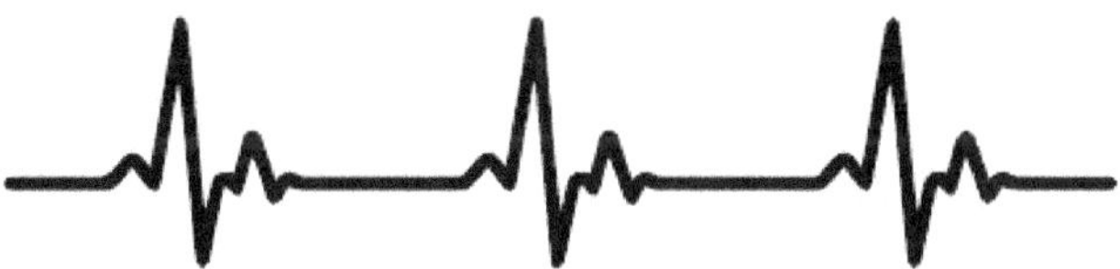

Control your own thoughts, control your destiny. This sounds so simple, doesn't it? Yet, it is one of the most challenging things for any person to do, and addicts take it a step further into the extreme. When Epictetus spoke of this, it would have been wonderful to pick his brain for more information. How can you control dark thoughts and put them into a healthy perspective? When controlling your destiny seems so self-absorbed, how can you do so with the best mindset? These are questions worth exploring.

These cycles of despair and hope offer plenty of perspectives that an alcoholic would be wise to contemplate. The basic themes of freedom, authenticity, and individual responsibility still exist. A need to explore them through the eyes of recovery and relapse must take place.

When I was going through these painful cycles that teetered on hope and then plummeted to new depths, it was never easy to see myself clearly and identify the downward slope I was on. All I could do was try and understand a bit more with each failed attempt during the enlightened moments—those aha moments where I did receive new clarity. I truly feel it is in these moments where hope is achieved. When things are looking worse for me, I've wondered if a person can have hope when they are not positive about the outcome. Is that even rational? It's a tough question to address; how would you answer this? I sense great importance in distinguishing between what is within our control and what is not. For so long, I grasped at the illusion I could control everything.

The harder I grasped, the worse I became. Imagine being a gardener with all the tools, seeds, soil, and water you need for a magnificent garden. Going to tend to your garden is a task you do daily—you control many aspects of the entire process. Your hope is to prune and harvest abundance. But then a storm comes along, and you encounter what you cannot control—the weather. It ruins what you've begun, and you'll have to start over next season. Unlike environmental seasons, the next season for an addict can be the next day. And that is a blessing to have this type of control available for the taking. We all have the need for seasons of healing and renewal. The beauty of this is the exploration phase, where you can find out why you need these periods of time and then take them. Explore your thoughts, grow your mindset, harvest your abundance.

Admittedly, I am not a great meditator to help with this, at least in the way I view it as being successful. I cannot sit tranquilly for even twenty minutes, which is why I chose to be more active in my meditation. I love my walks on the beach and touch with nature, which helps me realize what's important to me. In Buddhist views, they share an interesting concept, which is that you seek out the best for yourself. This concept shows life as a series of attachments that lead to suffering and are resolved by impermanence, not having to last forever. As an addict, impermanence is so meaningful because it helps you address the moment with mindfulness and a sense of detachment. Whether in recovery or relapse, seek a transient state. What's beautiful about this is it does not define our entire being. Who wants to be defined by our every action?

No one, I feel. Would you want to live the same life over and over again? Most of us who have an addiction would say no. However, we can use this type of thinking to imagine feeling that, yes, we would redo the life we've lived again. Recovery is the promise of a better life, and at the lowest moments, this awareness provides us with empowered thinking to change in ways that are pleasing to us.

Our identities are shaped by the stories we tell about ourselves. When we fill our thoughts with negatives about the way we act, look, think, feel, and even judge, we are defining our own story, and it is a tragic tale indeed. Addicts are vulnerable to being trapped in these narrative cycles. By reauthoring our narratives, we can place emphasis on qualities that are needed for a more robust life, one filled with resilience, self-love, and meaning. I cannot recall how many times I've tried to change my narrative, and it is finally working in small steps, but it is a lifelong pursuit I feel eager to take on. This is what I carry forth with in life. What is important to your life's progressions?

# 16 || Fire on the Horizon

*I've been through the fire, walked through the rain; felt the weight of the world, but I still remain.*
**—Stick Figure, Fire on the Horizon**

Big changes happen in the blink of an eye. What I experienced was impossible to process with a clear head. It was a fraction of time despite the story of my life flashing through my mind in vivid color and complete thoughts. I was curious to explore around me one second, and the next, I was toppling over a steep drop and heading down, down, down—a second that felt like an eternity. My bike flew out from beneath me and took its own trajectory to the bottom. A freefall like a rag doll, not able to put my hands out or do anything to stop the fall. All I could do was wait for it to happen. When I reached the bottom, the immense pain of a broken body took grip of me. Talk about a life changing fraction of time.

My intention had been nothing out of the ordinary, with ordinary at that time being drinking first thing in the morning. I had a simple desire to take a closer look at the ocean from that vantage point. I turned toward the right, leaving the main bike trail and veering onto the walking trail. I didn't slow down my peddling but felt I didn't need to. I was steady and in control, not even caring about any railings between me and the edge of that trail or even the 25' pit below me. Going at 20 MPH, I wasn't aware of the soft patch of sand on the path ahead of me, and I only realized it was dangerous when my front tire met with it. Control of my bike was lost, and I skidded out, literally flying right off the deep end. If the moment hadn't left me crippled from the impact and the pain, a surreal calmness would have surrounded me—that knocking on the door of death bliss that finally lets you know the pain is about ready to be over forever.

For several minutes, I lay there, trying to process what had happened to me. I was lying in a pit surrounded by rocks, hidden from everyone. Eventually, a fisherman saw me down in the trench and called for help. Every part of my body was either one that ached or was numb. Maybe I even passed out for a bit—I have no real idea of what was going on. When my eyes were open, they darted around, with my head barely moving, to check out my surroundings. Something shined in the distance, and I noticed my small flask. Some people never leave home without their Amex card, and I never left home without that flask. It must have flown out of my pack. In that moment, the dire straits I was in didn't compare to my need for what was in the flask. I stared at it through the blurred eyes which resulted from my drunkenness and agony. My hand slid over the sand and debris to reach it. I fell short. My body screamed in retaliation. No matter how hard I tried, I couldn't get to it.

I didn't realize how broken I was and that the flask was not mine to be had.

All I could do was wait to be rescued, and I hoped it would happen while I was still alive. This took so long, but I finally felt a hand on me, checking for a pulse. What a process this was. Only by reading the reports afterward did I know what took place. I was craned up by ladder trucks, and a crowd of onlookers gathered around—it was a dark day. When I was finally raised from the pit, the ambulance sped away with me, and my father followed behind it. Some wicked twist of fate had worked well for me that day, saving me again because if it had been high tide, I would have died. My body would have smashed against rocks, surrendering to them, leaving my lifeless body to be tossed about.

Once at the hospital, I was mostly passed out, on drugs for the pain. When I woke up, I couldn't remember any of the details of what I'd gone through for the most part. One thing I remembered clearly was the song I had been listening to when this happened. It felt haunting yet resonated as quite prophetic of my life and its many challenges. The song was one I'd known well then and know by heart today. It is Fire on the Horizon, written by John Gray and Scott Woodruff and performed by Stick Figure.

*There's a little old town*
*and it's tucked away on an island on the sea*
*So far away from everything*
*where time it don't mean a thing*
*And time moves slow and certainly*
*we got no place to be*
*Where's there's love there is life*
*there's a hope and a dream*
*This is the place for you and me*
*We can go, we can stay*
*We can hide, we can run away*
*We can feel and swim in the ocean*
*We've fallen, love keeps calling*
*I found love in the strangest places*
*where all is meant to be*
*Jamming to the sounds of your favorite song*
*I said good love is all we need*
*And when you get down, turn it up loud*
*and soon we'll feel at peace*
*When the world does you wrong, you listen to that song*

*like the birds, they listen to the trees*
*There's a fire on the horizon*
*There's a fire, so let it burn*
*We can get higher over the mountain*
*We've fallen, love keeps calling*
*In this jungle, we're all just animals*
*We're criminals, but we're innocent always*
*In this jungle, we're all just animals*
*We're criminals, but we're innocent always*
*So many miles I've walked*
*So many rivers I've crossed*
*So many battles I've lost*
*Make me who I am today*
*And when tomorrow it comes*
*There'll be a brand new sun*
*This song's not over*
*It's just begun*
*There's a fire on the horizon*
*There's a fire, so let it burn*
*We can get higher over the mountain*
*We've fallen, love keeps calling*

This song states quite well what my life and thoughts have endured. It has been a constant battle against the chaos, a desperate need to find calmness and clarity. The message in the words is intense and profound for someone searching for meaning in their life—someone like me. These lyrics are awakening to the senses and therapeutic to the soul, taking me past the physical parts of this accident, past my .29 BAC, and beyond the list of broken and fractured bones. These words helped me recognize all that was happening to me in such rapid order wasn't meant to be the end of me, as much as the end of one song and the start of a new one. This didn't mean I was sober yet, but I sobered up to some harsh realities.

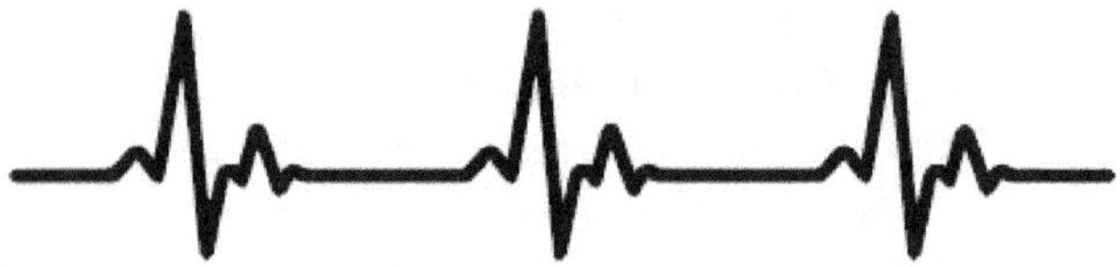

We all have been called to a battle in our lives, one that is ours to endure. Our results will either be to conquer it or fail at it as a result. A part of these lessons means we will be called to walk through the fire, which I view as our own defining moment of what our next steps will be. Since we all have a purpose, and once we realize this, the rain comes after the fire rages through, calming the inferno of our emotions, taking our hands, and helping us wash away what has weighted us down for so long. It renews our promise that there is more for us to do in this world. How do we know our story is not yet complete? We know because we are still here—we remain. Just thinking of this today gives me chills because it allows me to grasp how everyone struggles at some point in their life. Just knowing this takes me beyond the "me world" of an addict and into the depth of the human condition.

It feels like Fire On The Horizon (FOTH) was written for me. What songs make you feel this way and guide you through life by the power of their message, and how you are open to receiving it?

All the lyrics of FOTH have a place in my life and my recovery. At different times, the refrain or a verse will pop into my mind, reminding me to gain perspective and seek my true essence. Where the song mentions, "We can go, we can stay / We can hide, we can run away," has helped me to see that there was always an option for a different way, a choice to make that would guide me toward freedom or away from it. For too long, my choices had made me feel I was under constraints and restricted in what I could do because of my addiction and my low sense of self-worth. I'd lived my life with those low expectations for too long, always looking up at what I felt was a better life than what I'd created for myself. I just couldn't reach it for a hell of a long time.

My relationship with the world was more fractured than my body, all concepts of time and place lost within me if I even dared look past the bottle in my hand. How I longed for that "little old town tucked away on an island on the sea." That was the type of isolation I craved for both good and bad reasons. The good reason was I felt this pull from within me to reground myself and give me a new chance to do things better. The bad reason for wanting isolation was that I felt I wasn't worthy of trust, love, or goodness; suffering alone with my bottle was the best choice.

As healing started to begin (because I was finally willing to accept it), the way I viewed these lyrics to Fire on the Horizon gained new traction and became more personally empowering. Now, I can appreciate the beauty in those times, which moved slowly, as they removed me from the anxiety of my addiction and those situations that built me up to some of my most depressing times. Far too many days, I would have never believed there was a glimmer of hope, much less a light, at the end of this journey. How could my head space even process starting anew if I'd have to sink even further before I could begin? But alas, I have been able to do this, and it reminds me of the new journey—my new song—that is just beginning. Let me ask you, how do you keep going when you feel so unworthy of additional chances? We all should experience the power of love and life because that is what ensures we can still have hope and a dream. Although I didn't love myself, I knew love was a foundational, life-giving force available to me. Receiving love had never been a problem for me until I pushed it too far by pushing people away—friends, my wife, my children, and my family too. What a meaningless and sad existence it was to be alone because I was too afraid to do my personal work. I let go of my ex-wife, and by default, this meant releasing my sons as well. Have you ever found yourself in a situation where you are stuck—too afraid to heal? Too afraid to admit vulnerability? It sends you on a downward trajectory and takes everyone it can with you.

Compare this to love and how it gives life meaning, providing both hope and lending to the human experience. When FOTH repeats the refrain "love keeps calling," it is an emphatic reminder of how we mustn't give up. Sometimes, all it takes is to look up and know God is present for you. He helps those in need through the jungle of life's despairs and never stops loving us, even when we mess up. Where humans fall short is remembering this during our darkest hours. I know I did, and I was too embarrassed to even be near God. I felt certain He must be ashamed, a projection of how ashamed I was of myself.

It has been a long and arduous battle against myself and the physical part of addiction to start a life where I avoid alcohol and embrace self-love. It takes resilience and a sense of personal renewal each and every day. I love the promise of FOTH when they share: "And when tomorrow it comes / There'll be a brand new sun / This song's not over / It's just begun" because I know each day provides opportunity. Whether I make good use of it or fuck it up, the next day will bring with it the promise of a new chance for me. When I was drinking, I felt like a world record breaker for the number of days I messed up in a row—a many year long streak. I know I get to choose my narrative now, and it has helped me embrace authenticity and transformation in a way I've never experienced before. It's beautiful. We should all be able to fondly reflect on our lessons of transformation. I am finally able to look at my entire process and see something worth living a better life for. It's the promise of being in a better place for me, which will open up the invitation to reconnect with my sons and be the father they need, not the one they had for too many years.

Really, what the song FOTH brought to me in my moment of desperation that day on my bike was a powerful message. I shall always believe that we can have transformation through music. When I hear Stick Figure's rhythmic vibe telling me to jam to the sounds of my favorite music and that good love is all we need, I know that this starts with me and my perspective. I want to heal, and music is an important part of that. It's in my nature...and now it's a part of my nurture.

Just like my bike can be repaired from the mangle, so can I. This is the knowledge I carry with me today.

# 17 || The Two Million Dollar Man

*It is by going down into the abyss that we recover the treasure of life. Where you stumble, there lies your treasure.*
**—Joseph Campbell**

Shaking and trembling like a small child hiding from danger, there I was, a grown man, in the back of my parent's car. They were taking me to rehab one more time, hoping this would be "the time." I didn't blame them for their doubts because this would be my fifth attempt, the second at this facility. Despite looking like I was knocking on death's door, I felt different. Maybe the words had suddenly settled into my thick skull. My sister had told me she felt that her next big step to process would be my death. My brother felt certain he'd find me lying in my car, never to return again. As for my parents, the hell I'd put them through. Mom never knew what she might discover with me; my father had no more words that would get through to me. It was a waiting game… and no one was winning.

What I couldn't prove yet to those who doubted I'd be successful was how different this time felt. Something bigger stirred inside of me. Outwardly, I remained the same mess, digressing to even lower points than my mind had dared to believe were possible. Inwardly, I had finally admitted I needed to change for me, not for everyone else. This was a big step, one that I had never thought my fragile state would lead me toward, one where my very existence had been hanging on the brink of disaster. So much time, money, and resources had been put into helping me get better, from the physical accidents I had while drinking to the expensive attempts at rehab. It was no joke. I really was the two million dollar man…thank goodness for good insurance. The fortune of that doesn't elude my thoughts. Not everyone has been given these same options, but we are all given an opportunity for our personal best efforts. Thankfully, I no longer squander what can make me whole again; I care about what I'm doing, and it has made all the difference for this weary soul.

I said goodbye to my parents at the door of the Summit Estate Recovery Center, familiar with what would come first for me. It was the "blackout period," which meant no contact with family and friends. It would be just me, and the staff required to help me detox. To me, that was the scariest part because it made me as physically miserable as it did emotionally angered. Having been there before to know what I'd be facing didn't help because it was just that tough to go through the detox phase of rehab.

When I checked in, it was hard not to take note of my surroundings. They were so beautiful. This large circular house that would help me learn to help myself was affectionately known as The Ringhouse. It was surrounded by a mountainous backdrop, lush trees, and gardens everywhere. Inside the walls, I saw the promise of hope in a small, intensive setting. There were only six beds, and I was so damn scared for what I was going to go through, despite feeling how badly I wanted sobriety. Finally!

The road to sobriety isn't one a person can take alone, even though they need to put in the work because others can't change an alcoholic. Only the ones suffering can learn to make changes that are favorable for themselves. Being used to being a loner in my "condition," it was a big step to finally admit to the need for help. These people understood what I was going through and would help me address my unique needs as well. How strange it was to say yes to help and not suck the words back in after they left my lips. This declaration from me showed I was willing to open up to sobriety and get close to those who would help me. (Not that it didn't scare me senseless a time or two.)

Smiling and familiar faces greeted me. They did not mention me being there before. No "oh him again" looks. They were committed to me, and I was committed to the process. A new day, a new beginning. It was kind of fascinating to look at these people, they were such a cohesive team. It was another indicator of how fortunate I was despite looking like death had taken its toll.

Then the work began, an intense experience meant to heal my physical self as well as start me on the track to mental and emotional healing too. For those who have not been to a rehab facility, you don't understand an important part of the process, which is to keep you busy. The one I was at had me going 24/7, leaving little time to just do nothing. There were no moments to sit alone, unproductively, and let doubts build up about what you're doing. You are either in a one-on-one session, at the dining table, in group settings, visiting with the personal trainer, or doing homework. And that becomes life for at least the twenty-eight days you are there.

The immersion of so many types of therapy helped ensure we all had access to the types of tools and techniques that would benefit us most. And just as a carpenter has his tools to create, polish, and complete a beautiful woodworking project, we were provided with therapy tools to benefit us whenever we may need them. Music therapy, cognitive behavioral therapy (CBT), family therapy, psychotherapy, and even a Native American who taught us the philosophies of their people. There were days when I'd enter into these arenas with an open heart to make progress, only to leave feeling miserable. On other days, it was just the opposite. I'd enter there feeling miserable and leave with a new perspective. I'd try to meditate, and some days, it brought me solace and perspective, while other times, I was unable to calm my mind. These turbulent highs and lows were a part of the process, something I shouldn't feel competitive about and definitely not ashamed of. Focusing on shame doesn't help a person to heal and radiate a new light.

All the things offered to me were pivotal to my recovery. However, what I recall with great appreciation and love for my fellow housemates was the laughter we all gifted ourselves during these impactful days. Whether it was by our design or just due to decompression from years of addiction, we bonded over making a bit of fun of ourselves and our situations from time to time. Cracking jokes and embracing the absurdity of our lives. How strange it is to experience how this intimate and personal process blossoms with the help of others. The guys I experienced this with made a greater difference to me than I've probably ever let them know. We're still friendly today, and our "rehab message stream" is filled with some of the craziest commentary. It's blunt, heartfelt, and, most of all, encouraging.

Of course, the laughter we shared was often accompanied by streams of tears following it. The laughter built us up for the tough moments where we had to reconcile our actions and results to the choices we made to get there. How could you not create a bond with people you share such in depth emotions with? I never thought I would smile, much less laugh, in rehab, and the fact I did reiterates laughter can be a lifeline. This is what allows you to focus on more than rehab but your part in the world you have created for yourself. By focusing on the bigger picture, and not just rehab per se, it became easier to process certain problems better, learning to live life with others, free of alcohol. It's such a breath of fresh air, like inhaling deeply and smelling the salty air of an ocean.

My mindset began to shift, and while twenty-eight days don't fully heal, it opens up the audacity to dare to give yourself a new future that doesn't need alcohol. Starting to operate outside the "state of numbness" I'd lived in for so long was a catalyst for great expansion. What I learned about my mindset was that I just needed a new way to approach life, one that was cognizant of my authentic self. And what a journey it was to get to know that guy! So many thoughts, even more emotions.

Therapy was particularly important in reconciling the past to my new future in this arena because it helped me think about how I would approach life as a sober man. I sure as hell couldn't leave rehab the way I was when I entered into it for the fifth and last time. I contemplated new answers to pressing questions. What do you do when something goes wrong? How do you process it? How do you heal from an adverse event or accept it for what it is, which is something you cannot change? How will you address triggers that are no longer numbed by the bottle? What are the best ways to manage conflict with people you've hurt? These are just a handful of what was likely hundreds of these types of questions my wild mind had conjured up, yet they were all necessary to explore. When Albert Einstein referenced how you cannot solve a problem with the same mind that created it, it revealed just why those who devote their lives to helping people like me find sobriety are essential. Many of those who helped me had chosen to devote great parts of their day to helping me find sobriety, and some of them were addicts themselves—living on the free side of addiction for twenty or more years. So, no matter how alone I felt, I also knew they "got it." These amazing people didn't compare my experiences to theirs; they opened up their tool bag to help me in any way they could to understand the sources of my pain, the problems alcohol hid, just as much as the physical cravings of the bottle.

Recovery opened my eyes in so many ways, including all those easyouts ( the lies) I had created to justify my actions. Nobody was fooled in the long run, and those small temporary victories I claimed were attributed to so many falsehoods that got me through a moment in time. This had to change, and it isn't easy when you're in the moment of telling a lie to pause, speak the truth, and then move on. I've grown bolder when it comes to facing these shortcomings from the past, making sense of what has become distorted over the years, and trying to unravel the lies I sold myself on that simply are not true.

The lies are particularly hard for me because my boys suffered from my lies greatly, as did everyone important to me. However, I suffered most because I lost track of what was real and what wasn't. It was so muddled that I may never know about the past. I sure will know about the future because an honest assessment is a part of my daily reflection time. However, taking this bold step releases me from feeling like a failure because I no longer wish to live in lies but be comfortable with my truth. To do this, it takes a real conversation. The turning tide of recovery really cemented itself in my life when I finally embraced compassion. I have worked on forgiving myself and am mostly there. I've found forgiveness is one of the most liberating things you can do when you desire to heal. It requires introspection, which offers the hope of renewal to an addict. Gratitude lists have been important in finding life on the other side of forgiveness. And I'll be damned, changing your thinking really does change your life. I'm not a failed person, just a person with a few character defects and flaws, just as we all are. For some reason, alcohol was the catalyst that brought me to a place in life where I could acknowledge this wonderful realization.

I've awoken spiritually and am looking at life through a clearer lens. I talk about what I need, admit what bothers me, and am mostly fearless in my self-reflection of moments that cause me duress. If I sense fear, it becomes even more important for me to recognize why that is. This is all a part of me, and by honoring my needs, I am honoring my sobriety. It has enlightened me to this new side of life, and for that, I am grateful. This two million dollar man has come out swinging and sober.

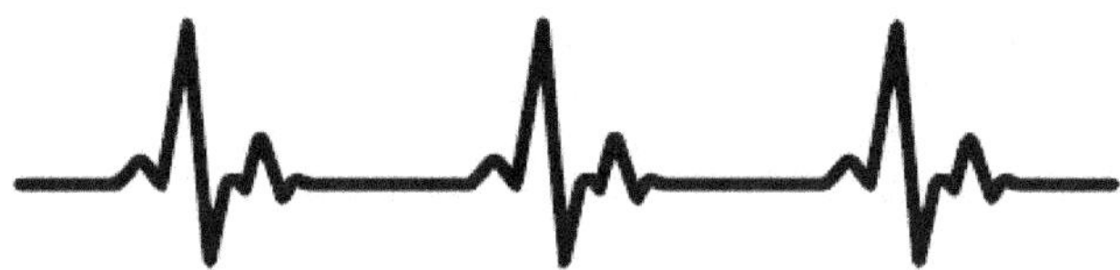

Joseph Campbell is renowned for showing the process of the "hero's journey" in mythology and revealing how it transcends into self-awareness for people to explore within their own lives.

As the quote at the start of the chapter suggests, it is through entering the abyss that we recover the treasure of life. The journey from active addiction to recovering addict is a hero's journey and one that has led me to explore the depths of my life, coming through the darkness and to the starting line of hope and a healthier outlook. This small win gives me a feeling of success, one which has been desperately needed for my psyche, if nothing else. What is success?

It is not mine to define it for others. For me, I do know success in sobriety will come from the sum of my small efforts. It's these little things repeated daily by me that lessen my desire to drink and make me realize how life is beautiful and worth exploring authentically and void of what takes me away from this better state of being. This awareness, combined with the experience of showing the upside to expressing my vulnerability, has awakened me to new opportunities.

Through recovery, a journey of self-awareness must commence. What did Socrates say? Oh, yes, "Know thyself." It turns out I'm not someone who should be living in shame and guilt. My character was never designed to hurt others, but I sure hurt myself. The motivations that carried me were ones where I craved to be a part of something bigger and better—whether it was me alone in nature or me in a room filled with people. It just required honesty and to embrace the "good, bad, and ugly" of my self-assessments to start making changes.

I didn't awake one day a whole new man; it was a transformation that carried bits and pieces of what was better for me and more true to me. I used the tools at my disposal to learn to use these and reconnect with a more genuine person.

How have you embraced those changes which could help you achieve another level of self-love and acceptance? Exploring this journey with sincerity and integrity will help you to find awareness about who you truly are. This is the starting point for those changes you may wish to see in your life. We are products of our existence, which means we have the opportunity to create who we are through the choices we make. For an addict, this can be earth shattering information, teetering on hard to believe. Then, you start to go through the steps of recovery, revealing your personal power to reshape your essence. With each drink you do not have, you give yourself the gift of time to engage in healthier activities and ways of thinking. Let your body become the brick foundation on which you stand strong, your soul guarded, your chosen way to live defined by what today brings, not what you surrendered yesterday.

When our past defines us, we trap ourselves into thinking the way we did when we were struggling. Who is it that wouldn't feel better if they were released from the constraints of past thoughts or events? These are all those situations that mill around our minds, not changed within our hearts but just destroying us from the inside out. Acceptance is the great liberator from these past burdens of the heart and mind. It is okay to accept what is not favorable from the past; moving onward is where we become our best selves. Starting now, we all can begin the process of becoming a changed person. The way we grow through addressing these adversities inspires me, and when I see it in others, I am amazed at what we are capable of doing for our personal greater good. I may still shake my head as I think about what has been done, but I also understand my head now, which is where I can be the repurposed person I have become, a man I love being. When we stop harming our character through the choices we make, something powerful happens: we become stronger. In recovery, we move from surviving with alcohol to thriving without it. Heaven knows there will be challenges, and that's okay. Each challenge conquered is a testament to resilience and finding comfort in our new skin. Realize what a gift this is to behold. It shows you've grown by developing virtues such as courage, temperance, and wisdom—qualities forged in the crucible of struggle. Knowing this makes difficult days more manageable.

When we enter this new space, challenges take on an empowering meaning. Yes, they feel unwelcome. However, they also demonstrate great potential to help you see firsthand how grounded you've become. The first time you don't overreact with words to an undesirable event is mind-rattling in quite a brilliant way. It feels good and helps you find the clarity to get you through the challenge.

These thoughts on how to live well are all made better when you have a supportive community. It would be unwise to think others can do self-work for you because it's an impossibility, an illusion. The value others bring to you is their ability to listen, encourage, and guide you toward your personal answer for what needs to be done. This sounds like an ideal friend, doesn't it? Look in the mirror, and you will also see another person who wants you to be authentic, accountable, and free from those life forces that deter you from building a better life.

# 18 || A Love Letter

*Being in recovery has given me everything of value that I have in my life. Integrity, honesty, fearlessness, faith, a relationship with God, and most of all, gratitude. Sobriety was the best gift I ever gave myself.*

**—Rob Lowe**

Being an alcoholic and having to take such severe action to address this debilitating disease was never in my plans. Yet, here I am, grateful for it happening because my road to recovery was also a journey of self-discovery. What I've learned about myself has changed my life for the better and made me more aware of everything that provides meaning in life.

Today, I can walk forward as a better man who is more compassionate and understanding. If I hadn't gone through this, I could not have been the example to others I would like to be. I understand grace and compassion, having experienced it from myself and from others, too. This has made all the difference in turning my troubling journey into something unexpectedly beautiful. Everyone around me can see it, which is nice, but I can feel it, which is amazing.

Alcoholism is a disease that impacts a swath of people, and many people suffer from the disease of one person. The trauma and embarrassment of that have been hard to work with, and to this day, I am still trying to reconcile this with my sons, and it will take time. I'm this new man, so excited to engage and be a part of this sober world that I sometimes forget, their caution isn't going to be equal to my enthusiasm for the journey. And I'm okay with this, still remaining committed to trying by demonstrating my changes. I understand their hesitation to take my word at face value. It has given me a sense of how deeply the wounds of betrayal lie for those who are affected by an addict.

Now, I reflect on the consequences of my actions to others without shame. My brother pleaded with me, on his knees, to get help. Remembering it has to be my choice to want sobriety helps; knowing I have this massive amount of love from my brother also helps. When my sister could finally share with me that she'd been forced to change her mindset from being able to help me to bury me, the depth of the pain she'd endured was evident—a sad reflection upon what I'd become, followed by joy for what she saw me evolving into. It's these moments your family was exposed to that can be the toughest to handle. They cannot unsee what they saw nor unhear undesirable words either. When I stopped beating myself up over those things and let self-love seep in, I was able to apologize to them for the pain from a genuine, heartfelt space. My actions were a byproduct of my human and faulty condition, and as strange as it sounds, like I mentioned earlier, my addiction led to gratitude on a more meaningful and profound level than I'd ever thought possible. My eyes are left wide open to the beauty on the other side of the darkness.

Needing more than alcohol has driven me to endure what I must to correct what has veered off course that I'd like to change. Again, reconnecting with my sons is the greatest example. It takes extra effort since they now live on the other side of the country. I may never have the bond I so desperately desire with them. However, I will always strive to make sure they have a glimpse into a person's life that takes accountability for their weaknesses. Hopefully, they will understand how taking care of their emotional garden will help them grow in miraculous ways. I cannot control their journey, but it will be a wonderful day if the line of addiction that has been in my family stops with me. What will my sons do? I wait with anticipation of their next steps.

Living life with a purpose is rewarding and fulfilling. This begins from the time I first open my eyes for the day. A task as simple as making my bed brings me joy because I have already accomplished something purposeful—I feel useful, and it's a more powerful way to feel than it might be credited for. The act of making a bed may be small, but it signifies a great deal more. It's a way to start my day on good terms, which lessens my chances of having an off day. These days are like the weed Creeping Charlie, enveloping you and leaving you in a struggle against the weed. We all have these types of days, and now I just have to live through them without the bottle in my hand. It can feel difficult, sure, but more importantly, it feels right to be sober.

A key difference maker for me has been being engaged with a recovery plan to provide me with the support I still need. And it is amazing to admit I rely on other people, minus the humiliation I once perceived myself as having an excess of. The people I've met in recovery, as well as my family and friends, want the best for me. They will be there for me, especially now that I am an active player in my fate. Before, I accepted a doomed fate without a desire to fight back against it. Once that changed, it was the start of my new beginning. Imagine taking your sunglasses off in the bright light; at first, it is uncomfortable, and you squint, but in time, you adjust, taking in the intrinsic nature of life through a brighter perspective. Brighter doesn't mean life will not have challenges; it does mean I will be able to see them clearer because I know myself better. All of this introspection has helped guide me to those sources that expand my knowledge and embrace the love that envelopes me. When I go to Mass on a Sunday morning, I find great solace in being there, closely connected with God and His word. I listen and try to absorb the message shared with me and leave His house with those messages in my heart. I strive to live better and forgive myself when I fail to do so, recognizing I am still God's child.

I've taken to life's higher meaning—enlightenment, if you will—to explore my connection with this world. In doing so, it has opened up my mind to the connectivity I have with those I love and anyone I meet. I see the potential behind people, not the plots sowing the seeds of their discontent. At the same time, I know to stay clear of those who are not a friend to my sobriety. I don't wish ill upon them; I just know I have to protect my wellness. It took a long time to get here, and it's a journey that is new enough that I'm not fully prepared to do more. I just feel grateful for what I can do, which takes me back to the blessings I've received on the other side of drinking.

# 19 || A Final Lesson From The Bottle

It felt fantastic to take an epic adventure to test my new sobriety, to prove I could live life without a drink, even if I were the only person around. No one else would ever know…except me, and I deserve better than to cheat myself again. I'd played that game for far too long.

I took a fly fishing trip to Argentina to connect with nature from my new lens. Everyone was opposed to me going. My therapists felt it was a decision being made too soon. But I was also aware of how I felt, and something compelled me to take the chance. To me, it was time, and I was craving the experience— what a change to crave an experience to better my life over the temptation of alcohol, so refreshing to my heart and soul. Since getting sober is both a journey of self-discovery and an exploration of the authentic self, I went.

Being in a foreign country alone and with a language barrier was a unique experience. I knew it was the type of environment I used to drink in—alone and in the wild. I also understood how my new appreciation for the world around me was a source of goodness, and I had every intention of honoring it as fully as possible. Time in nature will always be as wonderful as it is humbling. It was a great personal test to my commitment to this new life experience.

The journey began with me in Buenos Aires, attending Mass at the Metropolitan Cathedral, where Pope Francis used to hold Mass before becoming Pope. Inside this sanctuary for connecting to God, I found peace and beauty. It was a wonderful way to set up this trip. I also went to see a few other things in this country, one robust with its deep roots in Catholicism. This was the mental preparation for my time in the wilderness.

By the time I got to Patagonia for fly fishing, I felt prepared for what would lay ahead, in awe and reverence of the current of my heart, which felt its strong connection to all that surrounded me. I was a small dot consumed by God's love and the glory of nature. I'd never felt better or more prepared. When I cast my line that first time, I also cast out all those things which had previously stopped me short of participating in my best life. They were released into the water, and I was freed in the wild.

There is a poem called Fishing by A.E. Stallings that shows the nature of this relationship between man, life, and fish, expressing the transitions of life simultaneously. The words are a reminder of the fragility of life, nature, and finding meaning.

The two of them stood in the middle water,

The current slipping away, quick and cold,

The sun slow at his zenith, sweating gold,

Once, in some sullen summer of father and daughter,

Maybe he regretted he had brought her—

She'd rather have been elsewhere, her look told—

Perhaps a year ago, but now too old.

Still, she remembered lessons he had taught her:

To cast towards shadows, where the sunlight fails

And fishes shelter in the undergrowth.

And when the unseen strikes, how all else pales

Beside the bright-dark struggle, the rainbow wroth.

Life and death weighed in the shining scales,

The invisible line pulled taut that links them both.


If one day, my sons and loved ones can reflect upon my time in this world through this type of understanding of the connectivity of us all, regardless of where we are in our lives, it will show a difference has been made. I have endured what often felt like an impossible struggle, yet it was a path that guided me toward a renewed life which I am most grateful for. My experiences are better because I am authentic, and that couldn't have taken place without the darkest days of my alcoholism. This is perhaps the most powerful message to take away from Lessons From My Time With The Bottle.

# Acknowledgments

This book began with my desire to continue healing and share some of the insights that have driven me in wondrous ways on this journey. It has become so much more, and I want to acknowledge those who have inspired me in some manner.

To my sons. As these pages flowed from me, your images were the driving forces to keep me going. I am grateful.

To my circle of friends and family. Thank you for being a source to confide in, laugh with, and keep life real with.

To Summit Estate Recovery Center. Your caring and compassion for your work are par excellence.

To Jill McKellan. Thank you for your attentive ear and for helping me stay on task with this project.

# About the Author

Derrick How has written this book to share his lived experiences about addiction and recovery. These are more than just tales from the dark side, they are lessons from his time with the bottle—impact points that have generated a greater philosophical conversation about addiction and the individual. He is helping broken people understand their actions in ways which help them face their pain, hurt, and vulnerability. He knows how the other side of the disease has a more well-defined purpose and life.

It took Derrick well into his adulthood to finally reach his breaking point. And, like many people, it happened after several unsuccessful attempts at rehab. The road was laced with highs and lows, moments where he gave up, and plenty where he chose to be an unapologetic addict—stopping caring about anything and lying about so much, especially to himself.

A moment of self-actualization in Derrick's life opened up his receptivity to rehab. This time, he chose to go for himself—and it worked. He expresses that "the biggest difference in succeeding was I chose to change my path. It was for me, not for others." In turn, he has discovered the power of moving onward and finding peace in the process, whether it is fly fishing, contemplating, or golfing with a new desire to connect with the ball through the lens of appreciation, not competition. It turns out life holds gems to be explored around us and inside us, too. It's these insights that have provided Derrick with a renewed sense of purpose and clearer direction to follow, knowing he'll have challenges yet be willing to face them. He knows that day by day, strength can be found to tackle the beast that once destroyed life; we have the choice to move forward without feeding the dark side that created our chaos.

Today, Derrick has restored his optimism and knows his actions are what can make amends with his two sons. He understands there is still hard work to do, and when he hesitates, he finds comfort in God and with reflection. The biggest difference is he no longer fears his truths, even the uncomfortable ones. Connecting with a circle of friends with whom he can speak openly about his life provides hope and sparks on life's greater meaning—we need to connect with others to be at our best. In a sense, Derrick is reborn, and now is his time to extend the branch of hope for change to others who struggle with addiction or are impacted by this far reaching disease.

www.ingramcontent.com/pod-product-compliance
Lightning Source LLC
Chambersburg PA
CBHW071423150726
48000CB00001B/460